MARINE AIR
First to Fight

John Trotti
Photography by George Hall

Presidio Press ★ Novato, California

Published by Presidio Press, 31 Pamaron Way, Novato, CA 94947.

Library of Congress Cataloging in Publication Data

Trotti, John, 1936–
  Marine air.

  (The Presidio airpower series)
  1. United States. Marine Corps—Aviation.
2. Aeronautics, Military—United States. I. Title.
II. Series.
VG93.T76 1985   358.4'00973   85-3504
ISBN 0-89141-190-9

Printed in Japan by Dai Nippon Printing Co., Ltd.

Photographs by George Hall, with the following exceptions:
p.17, Robert Lawson; p.22, 24, 28, 29, 31, 34, US Marine Corps; p.64, Harry Gann/McDonnell Douglas; p. 99 (far right),
McDonnell Douglas; p.100, McDonnell Douglas; p.113, John Ficara; p.145, Harry Gann/McDonnell Douglas; p.146, Bell
Helicopter; p.154 (right), Nicky Wolf

Photographer's Note:
All photographs were taken with Nikon F-3 and FA cameras, plus a variety of Nikkor lenses ranging from 15mm to 600mm. Kodachrome 64 film
was used for color, Ilford HP 5 for black & white. Head and tail views in the air, such as the photo of the F/A-18 on the back cover, were taken
with radio-controlled Nikon FA cameras mounted in a remote underwing pod.

MARINE AIR

Contents

Courtesy of Mike Leahy

Dedication

Before dawn on the morning of October 25, 1983, members of the 22d Marine Amphibious Unit (MAU) awaited L-Hour, wary of the events that were soon to unfold but certain of their eventual outcome. The first of twenty-one aircraft composed of HMM-261's assortment of CH-46Es, CH-53Ds, AH-1Ts, and UH-1Ns began launch operations at 0320 in total darkness and rotten weather, forming up to deliver Echo Company (2d Battalion, 8th Marine Regiment) into Pearls airfield in the northern third of Grenada's eastern coast. It was the first heliborne assault against an opposing force since Marines went ashore at Chu Lai, Vietnam, in 1965. First over the beach was a section of Cobras tasked to reconnoiter the area and mark the landing zone (LZ) in preparation for the landing. At 0520 the lead division of CH-46s arrived at the LZ and began off-loading troops in the face of sporadic ground and antiaircraft fire, which was quickly checked by the Cobras. The remainder of the twelve transports—eight CH-46s and four CH-53s—entered and exited the zone at two-minute intervals, and by 0700 Pearls airfield was declared secure, freeing the transports to insert Fox Company into LZ Oriole, a soccer field two miles south on the southern outskirts of Grenville.

With two strong beachheads secured, the transports reverted to an on-call status, and the Cobras were released to support Army units at the south end of the island in the vicinity of St. George's Bay. The Army had previously landed on the newly constructed runway at Point Salines to rescue the medical students at the True Blue campus of St. George's University and had run into far more opposition than expected. It was becoming evident that Marine support would be needed on the south end of the island.

While reconnoitering the south side of the bay, one of the Cobras, Echo Mike Three-Two, was tagged by antiaircraft fire, most likely from a ZU-23 dual 23mm cannon lodged in a white building atop a hill overlooking the town of Belmont. The pilot was gravely wounded in the neck, arm, and leg, and the copilot was knocked unconscious by the concussion. With his right forearm all but severed, the pilot wrapped his leg around the cyclic (stick) to maintain a flare and brought in collective with his good arm to cushion the impact in the only suitable landing site in the area, a soccer field near the port facility in the middle of the bay. The superhuman effort left the crew members alive but immobile in the face of mounting ground fire that was beginning to zero in on the burning chopper. It was at this juncture that the copilot regained consciousness, released the pilot from his seat restraints, and dragged him away from the aircraft, whose smoke could be seen from halfway across the island.

From its station overhead USS *Guam* on the northeast side of the island, a CH-46 Sea Knight—Echo Mike One-Zero—heard the call for help and began a dash to the far end of the island to attempt the rescue. Rounding Point Salines, the crew sized up the situation, which read like a horror story.

Enemy troops had moved to within 200 meters of the wreck, and ground fire was coming from all sides. The flight path would put them directly under an antiaircraft battery on the cliff above the bay, and directly in line with the soccer field sat a Greek freighter. As the CH-46 set up for its ingress, Echo Mike Three-Zero, wingman of the downed Cobra, dashed in to look things over, noting that only the wounded crewman was now in evidence. With his 20mm cannon blazing away, EM-30 engaged the antiaircraft battery while EM-10 began his tortuous trip to the beach, close enough to the water's surface to ripple it on the way past. Holding low until the last moment, the CH-46 hopped up over the freighter and came to a stop fifty feet from the motionless pilot. The wheels were barely on the ground before the gunner had leaped from the plane and sprinted to the rescue. The volume of ground fire rose as the enemy troops closed the distance, and after the wounded pilot was aboard, the aircraft remained in the zone, hoping that the remaining pilot would emerge from the tree line. With enemy troops still advancing and EM-30 running low on ammunition, EM-10 was finally forced to evacuate the area.

With EM-30 again occupying the attention of the guns, the Frog (CH-46) pulled clear and exited along the same route as before, taking two hits in the tail mast for its efforts. Just as the CH-46 cleared the mouth of the bay, the Cobra was struck by ground fire, throwing it into a fatal plunge, where it struck the water steeply nose down, turned turtle, and sank. The toll for the action stood at three pilots killed (the one on the ground was found shot the next day), a fourth pilot recovering following the amputation of his right arm, and two badly needed aircraft destroyed.

Meanwhile, the battle was still going on. Late in the afternoon, Golf Company came ashore at LZ Fuels, just north of Point Salines on the enemy's flank, employing a classic amphibious surface assault. In what was becoming a highly fluid situation, fifteen aircraft—ten CH-46s, four CH-53s, and one UH-1—were sent to relocate Fox Company from LZ Oriole to LZ Texaco near Grand Mal on the western side of the island, where they could close with and support Army operations in the St. George's area. Through the evening and well into the night, transport helicopters cycled back and forth delivering men and supplies in anticipation of the upcoming day's operations.

The stiffest enemy resistance for the whole operation took place in the hills overlooking Point Salines. The ranger unit assigned to clear the area found itself pinned down, unable to mount an attack of sufficient strength to dislodge the enemy. October 26 kicked off with the insertion of Fox Company into a small clearing within Golf Company's perimeter that was hardly large enough for one CH-46 and too small to safely land a CH-53 at night. The operation was conducted in complete darkness, facilitated by the use of night vision goggles and a reliance on the pathfinding abilities of a UH-1 crew who directed traffic in and out of the zone, often resorting to the use of its searchlight to show the way. The last troops were landed by 0530 in what would prove to be the decisive move of the campaign, enabling the battalion to move toward the capital city of St. George's and link up with the Army.

While the sporadic fighting at Point Salines was still taking place, word was received that more than 200 American medical students and their families were barricaded in a dormitory building on the Grand Anse Medical College campus located three miles northeast of the tip of Point Salines. Nine CH-46s, four CH-53s, two AH-1s, and two UH-1s from HMM-261 were detailed to transport members of the 2d battalion, 75th Rangers (an Army unit), into a landing zone along the beach, rescue the American civilians, and return to retract the rangers. It seems simple enough in bare outline, but on that sultry Caribbean afternoon things were anything but routine.

In the first place, artillery and mortar fire from Salines had to be closely coordinated, as did attacks by a pair of Navy A-7s just prior to the push. An Air Force C-130 gunship was overhead, but like the A-7s, it could not be used once the choppers arrived. When the insertion began, the helicopters found the LZ (the beach fronting the campus) so narrow that the aircraft were forced to land parallel to the water, drastically reducing the amount of space within the zone. As a result, three of the aircraft sustained rotor blade damage, and although two were successfully flown out of the LZ, the third remained on the beach and was subsequently destroyed by ground fire.

From the outset, close air support was limited. Two Cobras had launched, but one was forced to return to Salines with a hydraulic failure. Using rockets, machine guns, and TOW (standing for tube-mounted, optically tracked, and wire-guided) missiles, the remaining Cobra made repeated runs against enemy positions, silencing those that held direct fields of fire over the LZ. Although the initial assault was masked by surprise, enemy resistance grew throughout the evacuation, and by the final stages of retraction, enemy mortars literally walked the LZ. The number of evacuees exceeded expectations, subjecting some of the aircraft to overloading. One CH-53 took off with sixty passengers, fifteen more than its limit—a condition calling for tremendous skill on the part of the pilot who was not comforted by the illumination of the tail rotor gearbox warning light. Because of the deteriorating situation at the campus, the last aircraft to evacuate civilians touched down directly in front of the dormitory, electing to risk a heavy dose of small arms fire in the process.

With the removal of the last group of rangers, the operation was successfully concluded. All 231 civilians were safe and unharmed. Three helicopters sustained some amount of damage, and one had been lost, but not a single crew member had been injured. From moment to moment things had been in flux. The crews had had to play it by ear from first to last, yet the mission turned out to be a resounding success, one that a thankful band of students will remember for a lifetime.

By the time that the last rotor blade stuttered to a halt, the battle for Grenada was effectively over. All that remained was the mopping up. Postmortems revealed that the operation had not gone as smoothly as expected, and it has been suggested in the sublime wisdom of twenty-twenty hindsight that some of the losses were perhaps avoidable. Mistakes and individual acts of heroism notwithstanding, what is infinitely more significant was the incredible involvement in and impact on the march of events by such a small number of aircraft and their equally small number of crewmembers and support personnel. It was the totality of the effort that carried the day.

With that in mind, we would like to dedicate this book to the officers and men of HMM-261, suggesting that their actions in the battle for Grenada characterize what has come to be expected of Marine Air.

John Trotti
George Hall
Novato, CA   July 1985

Preface

Folks, the ghost of Bull Meacham is alive and well. If you don't recognize him, it's because he's sporting a "no see 'em" paint job. The fact is that Marine Corps aviation itself is alive and well, with more things going on than you can believe. It's as if all the pressure that had built up in the restricted atmosphere of the Vietnam experience suddenly burst forth in a profusion of new ideas of roles and missions unmatched in the Corps's history. It's a wonderful story with its share of excitement and glamour to be sure, but beneath it is, as ever, a matter of people and hard work and commitment to principle and excellence.

There is any number of ways to see what's moving and shaking in Zoomieland. You could drop in and visit with the various commands that operate the equipment, or you could go to exercises in the field to watch them in action. You could walk around headquarters and talk to the program managers about what's happening, or you could sit down and read hundreds of different tactical manuals dealing with the multitude of roles and missions that Marine Air performs. You could do all these things and be greatly rewarded in the effort, but it would take you an awfully long time. The next best way is to let George Hall and me be your eyes. We'll show you the men and machines, their roles and missions, something of their past, what they are today, and a glimpse into the future. The magic of George's camera will take you where few have ever been—a sort of voyage into the eye of the hurricane—but that's not all. You're going to do

something no one has ever done. You're going to strap into every machine in the Corps's inventory and take it into combat. It'll be your hands on the stick and throttle as you hurtle into the target area at the speed of heat, kicking up a rooster-tail of cactus and sagebrush. It will be your eyes that pick out the speck that's an enemy fighter poised for attack. It will be your resolve that presses on in the face of blistering antiaircraft fire. In short, you've got the dot, so go for it!

To do this, we've created a magic carpet called "the scenario": a set of loosely knit events that evolve from a hypothetical situation. This isn't an unfair way to go about it. In fact it is the way the Marine Corps itself prepares for contingencies in various parts of the world—Europe, the Middle East, South and Central America, Africa, Asia.

There are plans and even pre-positioned stores and supplies that allow Marines to meet any of a hundred potential threats around the globe. The one we've chosen is a "brown side out" contingency pointed toward a desert environment such as that found in Africa or in the Middle East, but it could just as well be "green side out" or "white side out".

Imagine for a moment the circumstances: The first step is to establish a main operating base on friendly soil. An amphibious attack is then launched and Marines press inland toward the enemy's vital area. At some point, an austere forward air base is established, with aircraft, men, equipment, and supplies leap-frogged into position. A major battle is shaping up. It's all in place for you.

But before we go tactical, we've got a few administrative matters to address—background questions such as Why does the Marine Corps have its own little air force? (because they've got all those pilots hanging around, dummy); What does it take to become a full-fledged Marine hot shot aviator? (a thorough lack of understanding about what's going on); and What has Marine Air done in the past? (a whole bunch, thank you). It's a little like having to read all the standing orders when you check into a new unit, but we'll make it mercifully brief. Before anything else, we'd like to acknowledge a handful of people from among so many that to name them all would literally double the production cost of the book.

When you talk Marines, you start with the man himself—Gen. P. X. Kelly, twenty-eighth commandant, without whose blessings, I can assure you, you would be looking at a bunch of telephoto pictures and reading a collection of secondhand guesses. While you're still at the headquarters level, you single out Col. Jim McManaway of the Public Affairs Office for providing entree to the various operating commands, to Col. Ken Town for his insight into the overall structure and direction of the Corps, Lt. Col. Bob Soderstrom in personnel, and everyone in the aviation branch.

Out with the operating folks, things go from the ridiculous to the sublime. George and I dealt individually and collectively with more than a thousand people—officers, enlisted troops, civilians—in the forty or so units we visited, so singling out a few is a difficult task. To begin with, we never met a person who was unwilling to go out of his or her way to help. You see the word *unstinting* crop up in this kind of situation, and there's a tendency to dismiss it as hyperbole, but the truth is that in this case it is appropriate. In acknowledging the support of Maj. Gen. Clay Comfort and Maj. Gen. Keith Smith of the 3d and 2d Marine Aircraft wings respectively (the latter has since joined the Headquarters staff as the Deputy Chief of Staff for Air), George and I mean to include members of their commands, who received us so cordially. You know who you are, and we thank you. Brig. Gen. W. R. Etnyre, commander of the 7th Marine Amphibious Brigade (MAB) provided us with a rare opportunity to participate in CAX (combined arms exercise) activities, seeing to it that we had the best seats in the house. Much of the overall tenor of the book results from the advice of Lt. Col. Randy Brinkley and his dedicated band of gurus at Marine Aviation Weapons and Tactics Squadron One (MAWTS-1), who contributed many of the concepts displayed. Col. Myrl Allinder, my hootch-mate from Vietnam days and presently in residence at the Naval War College, played long-distance sounding board for the effort, injecting a fervor that I hope comes through.

As with the Marine side of the coin, one does well to single out the boss—publisher Bob Kane, the sine qua non before all others who has once again bitten the bullet with us. The jacket and layout of the book was handled by Lynn Dwyer and it speaks for itself. If there are better editors than Joan Griffin, neither George nor I know of one. And that about says it all.

It should be borne in mind that the book's focus on the aircraft as the means for showing the roles and missions of Marine Air is a matter of convenience for the writer, an editorial place to hang his hat. In reality, Marine Air is composed of elements that appear as thousands of line items in a table of organization. These are the people and things that transform the goals and objectives into action, and they do it in a fluid environment in which requirements can (and do) change in the blink of an eye.

Before the whine of the first turbine can take place, there must be fuel and LOX (liquid oxygen) and engine oil which allow a pilot to turn an assemblage of metal and plastic and silicon into a living, roaring, fire-belching weapons system. There must be the canopy cleaner and rags and elbow grease to ensure that the aircrewmen can see what they're doing. There must be the forklifts and SATS loaders and willing hands to hump the bombs and rockets and missiles. There must be the staff members to see to it that what needs to be there (be it man, machine, or material) is there, on time and in the proper condition and quantity. And it doesn't come close to stopping there.

There must be trainers and simulators and classrooms and people to man them. There must be cooks and messmen, heavy equipment operators and truck drivers, supply clerks and communicators and air traffic controllers and dozens of others who play a role in putting an aircraft in the right spot at the right time. To tell the whole story would take several volumes, but with George Hall's camera at the fore, we'll try to show you something of what Marine Corps aviation is about.

Chapter 1
MAGTF—Tasking for Success

Marine Corps. Just the name elicits some sort of picture for each of us. To some, it is of the flag-raising at Mount Suribachi; to others it is the march over snow-covered roads from Chosin Reservoir. To most of us under the age of fifty, it is of elephant grass and punji stakes; rice paddies and steaming jungle; Hue, Quang Tri, Khe Sanh, and An Khe—the abiding specter of ambush and pursuit that was the sobering reality of Vietnam.

Whatever the picture, it is tinged with that layer of esprit and devotion to duty that has come to symbolize the Corps since its inception and of which all Marines may be justly proud. But if the Corps's existence depended solely upon this, it would have long since ceased to exist. To be sure, the Corps is ever in the debt of the sacrifices of individuals, but often as not, these sacrifices have been made in the arena of policy. The facets that have in fact dominated the Marine Corps over its two centuries of service to the nation are those that are perhaps the least appreciated by the public at large: adaptability and innovation in the face of changing requirements, both of which have come about because of the vision and force of men, not committees. In no area are these traits more visible than aviation. Consider the following:

During World War I, Marine Corps pilots utilized aircraft in nearly every conceivable manner, including random and crude forms of close air support (CAS). But the use of air power for the direct support of ground forces by the Marine flyers in Nicaragua in 1923 was a far different thing. It was planned, coordinated, and repeatable, and the experiment marked as indelible a change in the battlefield environment as had the machine gun and tank in World War I.

In the fifties, after nearly a decade of improvement which had seen the helicopter grow from an oddity to a useful (if limited) tool, the Marine Corps introduced the doctrine of vertical envelopment, against the advice of most military experts. Even within the Corps opinion was divided, but the dedication of the true believers overcame opposition to the large-scale use of helicopters in combat, and today choppers are the backbone of assault work throughout the armed forces.

In 1967, a pair of Marine aviators walked into the Hawker Siddeley exhibit at the Farnborough Air Show in England and announced that they were there to fly the Harrier. Two weeks later, they were back in Washington, banging on desks, telling everyone who would listen how the Marine Corps needed the airplane. In-groupers don't have to be told how many times the AV-8 program has come within a whisker of being deep-sixed, but the program is at last a "go."

Nor will it end there. V-22 Osprey, the tilt-rotor offshoot of the XV-15 NASA test vehicle, is looming on the horizon. The Marine Corps, looking several years into the future, is spearheading the program, which aims to have a flyable prototype by 1987, and an operational capability by 1992.

Marines have had their own mini-air force for a long time, but with today's exorbitant cost of personnel and equipment, there are those who feel that it might be more cost effective if the Corps relied on the Navy and the Air Force for aviation support. To Marines it's a painful challenge, but a fair one. To answer it, one really has to ask whether we need the Marine Corps. The reason there is a Marine Corps is that it is a self-contained unit, capable of launching into battle with all of its supporting arms under a single command. The Corps is expeditionary, capable of conducting operations away from rear-echelon support. It is amphibious, able to deploy on short notice into every conceivable environment on the face of the earth. It is, in short, a round of ammunition, ready to be aimed and fired. Were Marines forced to go out to the Navy or the Air Force (or the Army for that matter) for support, these services would have to weigh Marine requests in light of their other priorities. At a crucial moment, assets might be assigned elsewhere, and that would be unacceptable.

Counting reserve, recruiting, and administrative birds, the Marine Corps currently operates sixteen different types of aircraft. This is nearly as many as the Navy or the Air Force operates, but it must be remembered that Marine Air handles all its own aviation requirements, except for nontactical airlift of troops and equipment—a service provided by the Military Airlift Command (MAC) of the U. S. Air Force.

At one time, it was convenient to talk about fighters and bombers and reconnaissance and tactical support aircraft as if they were unique entities, but the distinctions have become increasingly blurred as we push toward the last decade of the century. Some aircraft are optimized for particular missions for example the A-4s, A-6s, and AV-8s for attack—but the F-4s and now the F/A-18s are truly multimission machines, and if the RF-4s are to be replaced by the proposed two-seater F/A-18s, the Marine Corps could enter the nineties with a 97-percent common aircraft able to handle all its tactical strike requirements except those calling for STOVL (short takeoff/vertical landing) capabilities. But this is only part of the story.

Startling advances in the antiaircraft defenses of countries not generally considered to be highly advanced technologically have called into question the survivability of our aircraft over the battlefield. In Vietnam, attack helicopters became a valued tactical resource, and there is a growing suspicion that with their enhanced performance characteristics, helicopters could well displace fixed-wing aircraft in some aspects of the close air support role, if for no other reason than that their terrain-hugging ability affords them certain survivability advantages.

The outcome of the survivability question remains to be seen, but you can be sure that it will be constantly assessed. The need for close air support is just as great today as it was in Korea and Vietnam, so Marines will find a way to provide it regardless of the risks. Today's order of battle is itself an accommodation to a very fluid situation, and one would expect to see changes in black boxes, operating envelopes, and tactics long before the concept of the Marine air/ground task force (MAGTF) gets junked.

The seventies was a decade of crisis for the Marine Corps in general and for the aviation arm in particular. To begin with, the prestigious Brookings Institute proclaimed the Corps unsuited for anything but amphibious assaults against Third World opponents. Quite simply, its recommendation was to either pare the Corps to one and a half divisions or make it take on part of the Army's NATO commitments. The tremors had not even begun to subside at Headquarters Marine Corps, when the Israelis advanced the opinion that the days of tactical air support over the battlefield were numbered. A combination of clever aircraft dispersal and effective antiaircraft defenses prevented the Israeli Air Force from destroying its opponent's air resources on the ground, and for the first time since the beginning of Arab/Israeli conflicts, control of the skies had to be resolved in the skies. Postmortems brought to light several new "realities" concerning the tactical battlefield—especially those having to do with the accurate delivery of air-to-ground ordnance against heavily defended targets. The most frightening inference was that tactical air superiority over the battlefield of the future might well be a pipe dream. Ground-to-air weaponry was just too far advanced.

Marine Air was still in the doldrums—legacy of the Vietnam War, in which its role had been redefined by the U.S. Seventh Air Force under whose control all theater air fell after 1967. After several years of drifting and adapting to peacetime operations, Marine Air was ripe for a change, and the Israeli experience provided just the right stimulus. A conference was called in which officers from various levels and commands reviewed the lessons of the past few years and looked at alternatives for the future. The first issue before the conferees was whether there would be a role for Marine tactical aviation in the future. Clearly, if the answer had been negative, the Corps's very reason for existence would have come into question. The conference then addressed the issue of what the aviation environment would be in the future, and how to survive in the light of predictable and conceivable antiaircraft defense systems. Thus began a dialogue that exists to this day under the quasi-formalized cognizance of MAWTS-1, the Marine Aviation Weapons and Tactics Squadron.

Taking what might be loosely described as a systems approach to the problem, battlefield threat factors were teased apart and subjected to intensive and minute analysis. Considerations such as range, altitude, response time, and reliability were laid out and from these, generic threat parameters were established. Each was looked at in term of potential countermeasures, and certain generalities began to emerge. For instance, all things being equal, no-man's-land lies between 300 feet and 20,000 feet. Anything more than a quick excursion into this zone is almost certain to prove disastrous. Below 300 feet, terrain masking provides a high degree of protection, and above 20,000 feet, electronic countermeasures play a large protective role, but even these are not set in concrete. Speed is important, as is surprise, but these increase command and control problems, especially when communications are seriously degraded or nonexistent because of jamming. A whole new world was beginning to emerge and, within it a set of axioms that are even now translating themselves into hardware and procedures. The lethality of the enemy's antiaircraft weaponry is a function of the time it takes to bring it to bear, so that if you assume it takes X amount of time for the enemy to recognize, acquire, confirm, lock, fire, intercept, and destroy a target, anything that limits exposure time is desirable. Often, there is no one thing that, in and of itself, is capable of buying extra time, rather it is the aggregation of several things: surprise that causes a period of uncertainty; terrain masking that hides the aircraft for a certain amount of time inside the threat area; radar jamming that divides controller attention for a small amount of time; radio jamming that creates momentary confusion; aircraft jinking that adds complexity to the tracking solution; coordinated "roll-back" assaults that overwhelm the system; and attacks on the antiaircraft defense sites by nonaviation weaponry. These and many seemingly insignificant tactics help tip the balance in the favor of the attacker.

Determining threats and countermeasures is one thing. Dealing with them for real is another, and this is what the MAWTS program is all about. You can talk about blasting along at 475 knots just above the weeds all you want, but doing it is a different matter. To complicate things just a little more, consider having to reef the aircraft into a screaming 5 g turn to make sure there's no missile heading

for the poop chute. Add to that the chore of keeping oriented over unfamiliar terrain; throw in a little darkness or bad weather; add in switch management and timing, and you've achieved a monumental pilot workload. The only answer is practice. It's a step-by-step program designed to replace old habit patterns with new ones. Instilling in the pilot a sensitive appreciation for *time* is just a beginning. He has to learn to navigate precisely while constantly jinking in altitude, airspeed, and heading, all the while working to arrive at predetermined points at exactly the right time. Then he has to be able to maneuver his aircraft into position to acquire and attack the target with pinpoint accuracy. With all the increases in aircraft capabilities that have occurred in the wake of Vietnam, the mission is, if anything, more demanding than ever before. Every new refinement to on-board equip-

ment instituted in an attempt to cut the pilot workload is gobbled up by the exigencies of the mission. Fly lower. Fly faster. Cut down on the length and duration of the ordnance delivery run. And it is not simply a matter of stick and throttle. It is technique. It is tactics. It is coordination and teamwork. But there is one thing more, and that thing is a sense of mission. It's a subtle thing, but it's what allows a Marine ground commander the luxury of knowing that if there is any possible way for his troops to receive air support, Marine Air will provide it.

MAWTS-1 is located at MCAS Yuma, and though it resides on 3d Marine Aircraft Wing (MAW) turf, it belongs to (and is funded by) Headquarters Marine Corps. Thus it is a Marine Corps wide asset tasked with upgrading the knowledge and skills of all Marine aviators. It does this

Previous Page: Flight of A-6E Intruders prepares to launch into a patented Cherry Point all-weather sky.
Above: F/A-18 Hornets of VMFA-531 tighten up for a vertical formation turn over the Pacific coastal fog.

with a variety of programs including supplementary courses at the Corps's Amphibious Warfare School and Command and Staff College, but the most visible is its WTI (weapons training instructor) course. Held twice a year, the seven-week WTI course is an advanced post-graduate school of sorts, where people from all the different aviation units are subjected to the most comprehensive course on aviation threat analysis and tactics to be found anywhere in the free world. Prerequisite for fixed-wing pilots is the U.S. Navy's "Top Gun" fighter/weapons school at Miramar Naval Air Station, and nearly everyone has had experience at the various major exercises such as Red Flag hosted by the Air Force at Nellis Air Force Base. Not just aviators attend WTI, but air control and antiaircraft missile people as well. After classroom instruction in threat analysis, aircraft roles and missions, weapons systems employment, aviation training management, and integrated operational planning, the students take to the air to practice what they've learned, including the less glamorous tasks of demonstrating the ability to conduct proper briefings and debriefings and apply incisive airborne instruction techniques. At the end of the course there is a combined tactical exercise called Finex, in which infantry, armor, and air units get together and have at it. What emerges from the program is a new crop of WTIs who then take their knowledge and skills back to their units to be passed on to others.

Another goal of the program (beyond the creation of individual skills) is standardization. The idea is not that Marine aviators become a bunch of MAWTS clones, but that they learn to subject their missions to critical analysis, sorting out what's important from the fluff. If you can brief a flight completely and properly, addressing the areas of risk versus return, there is a chance for successful completion of the mission. When you begin to realize that there are different ways to accomplish a task and that some are better than others under various circumstances, you see that standardization doesn't mean conformity, but alternatives of action—and you can never have too many of these.

So successful has the program been that both the Army and the Air Force have requested quotas for the WTI program (providing exchange tour instructors as collateral), and the Navy, with it's Strike Warfare Center under development at NAS Fallon, Nevada, is heading in the same direction. If the course does nothing more than foster an understanding of the capabilities and limitations of the various aircraft and equipment, it will have more than paid for itself. The real goal, however, is to produce people who can go back to the operating units and fire up their squadron mates with an enthusiasm not merely to "hack it," but to excel.

Unlike the other services who see air in terms of specific ends, Marine Air (no more or less than artillery and armor) has always been perceived of as being there to support the infantry. The final authority for the employment of air lies with the ground commander, but it is not so much the one-sided affair it once was. For years, the attitude of grunts toward zoomies was summed up by the oft-vocalized barb "We understand why you guys get flight pay. It's the base pay we don't agree with." Technological advances, coupled with a better understanding of our experience in the Vietnam War, have enhanced the Corp's approach to combat substantially, and the role of aviation has grown. Battlefield intelligence gathering and real-time information processing and dissemination are just a part of this expansion. Factors relating to mobility and firepower have provided Marine Air with new frontiers, and with the steady rise in enemy antiaircraft capability, new tactics and equipment have been adopted to promote an acceptable level of survivability in the increasingly hostile environment. The proliferation of smart weapons, which have given rise to pinpoint accuracy has permitted new tactics that allow the attack aircraft to get on- and off-target with minimum exposure. Yet this is only part of the survivability situation.

With the continuing advance in antiaircraft weaponry, and the recognition that never again can we assume we will have free reign of the skies over the battlefield, infantry commanders have had to look more closely at how their tactics and weapons match the capabilities of their aviation units. Increasingly, operations are being conducted under the cloak of darkness and/or inclement weather, and awareness of these emerging realities in the conduct of tactical warfare has led to fundamental changes in the structuring of the Corps's task elements. One result is the MAGTF, which is the real focus of this book.

At 600 knots an RF-4B reconnaissance jet can be overhead and past well before its shattering sound crashes down on any who might be below. Hugging the earth, the photo bird is a blur of motion for just an instant before it sweeps out of view, leaving in its wake a trail of dry thunder to echo its passing. Within minutes, the plane will be back on the ground, its film processed and ready for interpretation. In time of war, the timeliness of such vital information can make the difference between annihilation and success. To the Marines taking part in a CAX (combined arms exercise) it is no less critical.

At the top of MAGTF's command and control loop is the fire support command center (FSCC), which is staffed by representatives of the various supporting arms elements—air, armor, artillery, and naval gunfire—and is under the direct control of the field commander in charge of the operation. It is the nerve center through which intelligence of the enemy situation as well as friendly units' disposition and status flow. Not only does it assist the planning staff by offering options, but it coordinates the actual strikes themselves.

In a typical scenario, information from various sources filters through the FSCC. A reconnaissance flight is one method for gathering intelligence, but with the dramatic increases in sensor and information processing technologies, there are others of increasing value as well. Things that are important to the decision maker are the timeliness, accuracy, and detail of the information. Often, a single overflight is not enough. Succeeding reconnaissance flights using a variety of sensors might be launched to bring back additional data, providing an ever clearer picture of the situation for the planning staff. As data accumulate, objectives can be more fully defined and even specific targets determined. It is stunning how many changes have occurred in the short period of time since the Vietnam War, changes wrought in the main by those little bits of silicon that provide Pac-Man with his insatiable appetite for dots. The microprocessor chip has brought about a revolution in many areas, but in none perhaps as notably as in the C^3I (command, control, communications, and intelligence) area.

Mounting an assault is anything but a trivial exercise. It is in the ability to control and coordinate the activities of the various elements of the MAGTF that the success of an operation lies. The unprecedented mobility of the present-day Marine Corps is at once a blessing and a curse. In a fluid environment, timing becomes increasingly crucial, and though communication equipment is spectacularly better than even a decade ago, the problems of coordination have grown apace. To begin with, with so many more communications taking place, frequencies are often clogged. After jamming, terrain masking, and atmospherics have taken their toll, misunderstandings and human error add to the potential for error. Under the best of circumstances, effective C^3 is an iffy business, but the Marine Corps's resolve to press on in the face of uncertainty and hardship opens the way. For certain, good equipment and determination are important, but not half as important as realistic training in which all the task elements are involved.

The CAX is one of a number of such training exercises, but it is particularly significant in that it points up a fundamental change in how the Marine Corps intends to carry out its mission in the future.

A MAGTF can be constituted any number of ways: from a battalion and a squadron at the low end of the spectrum to a division and an air wing at the other. The 7th MAB (Marine Amphibious Brigade), headquartered at Twentynine Palms in the California high desert, consists of a reinforced regiment, armor, a maintenance and repair unit, and a composite air group combining the various categories of support aircraft. Currently, the MAB is able to deploy on short notice and rendezvous with any of several pre-positioned supply caches in a secure area. From there it would proceed to mount an assault to seize and secure an advanced base.

Periodically, elements seconded from major Marine Corps commands arrive at the "stumps," eager to test their mettle in what has come to be one of the most comprehensive live-fire field exercises in the free world. The central unit is typically a reinforced infantry regiment joined by a provisional Marine Aircraft Group (MAG) drawn from assets of the 3d Marine Division and the 3d MAW respectively. Why they are here and what this all means are not as obvious as it may at first seem. A CAX is a live-fire exercise to be sure, but it is more—much more. It is at once a glimpse of what the Marine Corps is today and a harbinger of things to come. The Marine Corps is in transition, and in concert with the 6th MAB at Camp Lejeune, the 7th MAB is at the cutting edge.

A CAX is practice, but it is played live and at full volume, and while the exercise is "canned" insofar as its physical movement is concerned, it holds many of the surprises of a real war. Typically, it kicks off with a flight of A-4s passing east to west at low altitude dropping smoke to mask the deploying troops and armor. During the next three hours, in which participants experience the transition from the bone-chilling cold of dawn to the strength-sapping blast-furnace that is the most memorable characteristic of mid-morning Twentynine Palms, aircraft under control of MAG-70 (a provisional Marine Aircraft Group staffed by MAG-

13 personnel) continue to pound away at targets blocking the objective for the first day of battle. In the lead tank, a forward air controller (FAC), fights to keep himself oriented in the shimmering heat. He is one of two assigned to the ground troops from an operating squadron in what is known as the "Rent-a-FAC" program to coordinate close air support. His call sign for the exercise is Whiplash.

Ahead, a recon patrol sights two junked vehicles representing enemy armor lying in defilade behind the banks of a dry arroyo. Their position commands the main force's intended route of advance. The information is relayed to the TFSC which in turn passes the requirement on to the DASC (direct air support center) for action. The DASC is a dimly lit command post with status boards, radar consoles, and communications stations. It is here that the various aviation assets are monitored and assigned as necessary to specific targets. In this case, a pair of F/A-18 Hornets carrying seven 500-pound bombs, airborne at a preassigned OP (orbit point), is tasked with the mission. The flight leader calls his wingman to the strike frequency and checks in.

"Whiplash One-Four, this is Condor, over?"

"Roger, Condor, this is Whiplash One-Four. Say your position."

"Condor is a flight of two Fox Alpha-eighteens orbiting Lima at base plus six-point-five with fourteen Delta-twos for your control." Condor is informing Whiplash of his location, ordnance load,

and altitude, the last referenced to a prearranged code (today's base altitude is minus 2,000 feet, meaning that the flight is at 4,500 feet above sea level—1,500 feet above the desert floor and well below the mountains).

"Roger, Condor. Are you ready to copy your mission?"

Going quickly down a standard checklist of information, he provides details on the mission to the Hornet pilots, while seven clicks (kilometers) to the north, a lance corporal, concealed in the sparse underbrush along a hillside, readies himself to illuminate the target with his MULE (modular universal laser equipment). From his position he is looking down the throat of the enemy armor. It's a matter of timing. If the target illumination commences too early, it will give the enemy a chance to combat the MULE or perhaps destroy it altogether, but if it starts too late, the strike aircraft won't be able to pick up the target, exposing themselves needlessly while committing themselves to a second pass.

"Whiplash Two-Seven, this is Whiplash One-

Below: RF-4 makes low-level photo run at the "speed of heat."

Right: Radar controller in TACC (Tactical Air Control Center) on mountaintop overlooking Twentynine Palms.

Four. Commence target designation," the FAC orders over the VHF (very high frequency) net to the MULE operator, and then to the inbound aircraft over the UHF (ultra high frequency) radio he informs, "Condor, this is Whiplash. Stand by for designation."

On the brow of a small hill, the battalion commander peers intently at the tanks through his binoculars, anxiously awaiting the arrival of the jets. He never sees them. In fact, in recounting the incident he was not sure what it was he did see—just a blur and then a tremendous mound of dust where the lead tank had been, and before the pall settled, a sharp report followed at some length by a second geyser. Away to the south, he heard the tearing roar of a rapidly retreating pair of aircraft. The sound rose and fell for a moment and then was gone. Both vehicles had taken direct hits without his ever having laid eyes on the attackers.

Using FLIR (forward looking infrared) receivers the Hornets had done their job. The practice attack had gone off the way it should have (and why shouldn't it with all the expensive and sophisticated gadgetry involved?), but the impression it made might have been more important than the mere removal of an obstacle. One of the aims of the CAX is for members of the various elements to come to know and respect the strengths and weaknesses of one another so that some day on some foreign beachhead with life and death in the balance, Marines will act in concert.

This isolated air strike could have come off in a variety of ways, depending on the situation. Instead of a recon team on the ground, the target could have been spotted from the air by a reconnaissance jet or an observation aircraft, in which case control of the strike might not have been in the hands of the FAC. The attackers might have had to locate the targets themselves or with the help of other aircraft, perhaps an airborne laser designator mounted on an OV-10. Maybe the antiaircraft situation and terrain would have favored the use of AH-1Ts using their TOW wire-guided missiles. If the enemy had antiaircraft guns in the area, artillery fire might have been used to engage them to provide a corridor for the strike. There's more. EA-6s might have been used to jam enemy radars, A-4s might have saturated the area with chaff, smart weapons containing terminal guidance might have been lobbed into the area and left on their own to seek out and destroy the targets. The point is that every target situation is different. In combat, there are going to be losses, but the flexibility to use the best tactics under the circumstances can help prevent them. This is why the Marines have such an incredible mix of aircraft in their bag.

Chapter 2
The Airdale

There is a mystique surrounding the Marine Corps that has grown over the more than two centuries since its founding in Philadelphia on November 10, 1776. The word most often used to describe it is esprit, the embodiment of the "can do" spirit. Ask a Marine to jump, and he'll answer not "huh?" but "how high?" Few would ignore the awesome achievements of Marines at Belleau Wood, Tarawa, Iwo Jima, and Inchon, and while they have not been accorded their true place in lore, there are dozens of campaigns fought in the jungles and elephant grass of Vietnam that deserve recognition as well. If it can be said that no Marine rifleman need take a second seat to anyone, what then of the Marine aviator? How does he measure up?

To begin with, the distinction between the various air arms is primarily a matter of mission. The Air Force's tasks range from global, at the far end of the operating spectrum, to theater-wide at the other. Thus its attention is drawn to rather large matters that lie more reasonably in the region of numbers and probabilities. Naval Air provides fleet support including such diverse specialties as antisubmarine and antisurface warfare, fleet air defense, air superiority, and air-to-ground interdiction strikes. In the last category, the Navy, like the Air Force, thinks more in theater-wide terms, tending toward the "big event." Army Air is composed almost entirely of helicopters used for the deployment and direct support of infantry operations. Thus in its rotary-wing mission it bears a marked similarity to its Marine counterpart.

In comparing themselves to others, Marine aviators will usually begin by listing the virtues they see in their contemporaries. Professionalism and tremendous knowledge are factors most often brought to the fore. In the case of the Navy, carrier operations and fleet air defense are acknowledged superiorities. The Air Force's ability to conduct deep interdiction raids and to achieve and maintain air superiority over large areas are viewed with admiration. Army pilots are hailed for their success in being able to move large numbers of men and equipment into a landing zone quickly. What then do Marines see in themselves that is significant?

In a nutshell, it is flexibility, a responsiveness that results from the knowledge that their role is not the be-all and end-all of the show, but rather that of a supporting element. Mission, "can do" spirit, and teamwork all make their mark, but there is within the body of Marine aviation the unspoken premise that, though discipline in the air is important, it should not be so rigid as to curtail creativity in dealing with real-time situations. Thus, Marine aviators assume they are on the longest tether of all the services, and it is probably true if for no other reason than their belief it is.

The image of the Marine Corps aviator is in flux, and to a certain extent it depends on the beholder's age. In World War II, Pappy Boyington exemplified the Marine fighter pilot. Tough, grisly, spoiling for a fight, the Corps's ace of aces was (and is) a true original, and as his image fades with the changing times, there are many who rue its passing. In the early jet days, the image shifted to the Ted Williamses and the John Glenns. Today, for the most part the Marine aviator is faceless, in keeping with the Corps's desire to maintain a low profile. In some ways he's different from his predecessors, and that's as it should be. In general, he's older, more mature, better educated, more self-disciplined, and more rounded, and if this makes him sound like a goody-two shoes, some of that too. But underneath, there is the same zealousness that has been the hallmark of Marines since A. A. Cunningham made his first solo more than seventy years ago.

Time was when many Marine aviators were enlisted, some throughout their entire careers, others at least until they graduated from flight school, where they received their wings and commission at the same time. Today, all Marine aviators or flight officers go through Officers Candidate Course or Platoon Leaders Course and then Basic School at Quantico, Virginia, where they are taught about duty, sacrifice, teamwork, and all the attributes and principles one ascribes to the Marine officer. But what they are really learning is "semper fi." Semper fi (short form of the Corps's motto, semper fidelis, meaning "always faithful") is not a code that tells Marines what they must do; it is not a series of textbook solutions that lead to some inexorable mode of conformal behavior; it is an attitude that allows them to do what they must. More than that, it is a spirit that once inculcated becomes a living, driving presence. To say that the Quantico graduate is a fanatic is not putting it too strongly, though Marines themselves prefer the word esprit.

Quantico is the crucible. After serial trips around the obstacle course, interminable gut-wrenchers up and down the Hill Trail, nightly opportunities for locker box drill, unceasing drill sessions on the grinder, sleep-inducing lectures on how to construct a one-two-three trench, the rigors of the confidence course, the nerve grating "I can't hear you,"

Above: Pilot runs pre-start checks in VMAQ-2 Prowler electronic warfare bird.
Right: VMFA 323 Hornet receives anti-corrosive wash job at El Toro.

the pugil sticks, and umpteen thousand different skirmishes in the boonies, the graduate comes away . . . *different.* There's just no other word for it. He's looked into himself and found new depths. He's tested himself and found himself able. He's challenged himself and grown to new heights. The vision he takes with him to Pensacola for flight training sets him on the road to becoming a breed apart from his newfound companions of the "Brown Shoe Navy." When he graduates some fifteen to eighteen months later, the speciation is complete, as indelible as the uniform that distinguishes him.

There are four phases to the Naval Air Training Command: preflight, primary, basic, and advanced. Within each phase there are numerous stages in which the student is introduced to specific tasks. After primary training, students become speciated, proceeding through pipelines that will lead them to jets, props, and, in the case of the latter, perhaps helicopters. Regardless of the pipeline, all aviators learn not only the basic flying skills, but those peculiar to the Naval aviator—bombing and rocketry, air combat maneuvering, and carrier qualification. The training command is the place where a large variety of flying skills and thinking patterns are imparted to students whose only responsibility is to absorb the information and then perform in an acceptable manner. Although there is a sense of urgency and a pressure toward perfection, it is more like college than what is to follow. Though the training may have prepared the student for a specific task, it is general enough to allow him to make the transition to other aircraft and other missions as the needs of the service dictate. He is, upon graduation, a competent pilot, but a long way from being a complete aviator.

As soon as he has completed the course and received his wings, the fledgling is given orders to one of several Marine training squadrons located on either coast. There he will make the transition to a fleet-type aircraft and focus on the skills that will allow him to perform the specific mission for which the aircraft was developed. For helicopter pilots, it might be HMT-301 at MCAS Santa Ana, California, or for fighter types, VMFAT-101 at MCAS Yuma, Arizona. The Marine Corps supports training squadrons for each of the tactical aircraft it flies (except the EA-6, which is handled by the Navy at NAS Whidby Island, Washington), and though the training cycle varies from aircraft to aircraft, the new pilot will spend in the neighborhood of three months getting checked out in the "type" airplane he will fly when he goes to a fleet squadron. At the end of this time he will be roughly 60-percent qualified.

In all military aviation, the squadron is where

the action is, and the Marine Corps is no exception. From the first time he sets foot into the ready room, the new arrival is caught up in a world that is more encompassing, more overwhelming than anything he has ever experienced. Externally, a squadron is a collection of equipment and skills standing at the forefront of a hundred activities that comprise Marine Air. It is the cutting edge where the cumulative efforts of thousands pay off in the accomplishment of the mission. Viewed from afar, it's the place where the noise and smoke and confusion sort themselves out into close air support or air superiority or troop emplacement or photo reconnaissance; indeed, any of a dozen other missions performed by Marine aviators.

From within, the squadron is far more. In fact, to the first-tour aviator, it is (except for the time spent at a few schools here and there) the whole world. Something might be happening across the street, but it doesn't matter. Family, friends, fraternity all pale by comparison to the demands levied by the squadron. It is about as subtle as a whorehouse, establishing rules and guidelines for nearly everything the squadron member will do until he leaves for a new assignment. And even then he takes the squadron's attitudes and assumptions with him, an indelible emblem of his tenure. If you know what to look for, you can distinguish between someone from VMFA-314 and someone from VMFA-323, even though they're part of the same air group and they fly the same airplanes. It's the words and gestures they use for one thing, but there's something in the body language as well.

At first it's a sensory overload, but after he gets over the initial shock the neophyte is drawn into the day-to-day life of the squadron. If you think it's all flying, you're wrong. Likely as not, the first thing that happens to a new arrival is his assignment to a collateral duty. Often this is a collection of minor functions such as fire marshal or Navy Relief Drive officer or buildings and grounds officer. All are necessary, having to do with command policy or reporting requirements, and the manner in which they are performed will be carefully noted. Usually no one job is too demanding in and of itself, but aggregated they become a full-time occupation. Add to this his various watch-standing duties and outside assignments, and he's into overtime. There's another dimension to it as well. The aviator is first and foremost a Marine officer who can be called upon at any moment to take command in almost any situation. Because of this, the Corps needs to know not merely that this person can manipulate a stick and throttle, but that he can measure up to other demands as well. In writing the fitness report, the commanding officer leans heavily on performance of his primary duty as an aviator, but promotion boards (composed principally of ground officers) will study the other categories with keen interest.

Flying is prime time, but it almost gets lost in the welter of activities that go into the accomplishment of the task. First, there's the foreplay—the studying, planning, simulator training, briefing, and preflighting. Afterward, there will be postflighting and debriefing. The duration of an average flight is around an hour and a half, but when you add in all the preparation and wrap-up, the involvement comes to nearly three times that. "Boot" or "old shoe," junior man or commanding officer, everyone in a squadron lives on borrowed time. The fact is that life in the squadron is so hectic, what with exercises, inspections, deployments, dog and pony shows, and the almost daily Chinese fire drills, that an entire tour goes by in a blur. One instant you're checking aboard, and the next time you look around, you're heading out the door with a new set of orders.

Typically, the first brief begins an hour and a half before sunrise, and those who live close to a base can attest to the fact that the first launch is a good indicator of when the sun is about to put in an appearance. By 0800, all hands are aboard, and for squadron officers not otherwise occupied, there

Clad in ''no-see-'em'' paint job, Yuma-based VMFAT 101 Phantom banks toward the Camp Pendleton range on an air-to-ground training mission.

is a meeting during which administrative information is passed along. Routinely, flight ops continue far into the night, and while administrative sections generally secure for the evening, the maintenance effort is often an around-the-clock affair. Shop personnel are divided into watch sections (wings), arriving and departing in overlapping shifts, so that periods of inactivity in the squadron area are rare.

Squadrons spend a great deal of time on deployment. Sometimes it's for routine training to take advantage of special facilities such as the ACMR (air combat maneuvering range) found at MCAS Yuma. The proficiency gained in the concentrated flight training is one thing, but the truth is that these little deployments offer a number of side benefits that help to jell the unit and prepare it for larger moves. To begin with, there are several weeks of preparation during which the goal is maximum availability of aircraft and equipment. Toolboxes are readied; test equipment is calibrated; little things

that have been allowed to slide are fixed. With this, a sense of purpose and anticipation begins to grow. Concurrently, things move into high gear in the various office spaces.

The operations staff draws up detailed plans for the flyaway and for activities during the deployment. A liaison is established with the various host commands. Target times are arranged, procedures checked, radio frequencies determined, ordnance ordered. If there is to be an air-to-air missile shoot, missiles and targets are requisitioned. Range and launch support commands are contacted to confirm their availability. There always seems to be one more thing: air refueling tankers, block altitude assignments from the Federal Aviation Agency, weather forecasts and briefings, barracks assignment, messhall availability, motor transport, and so forth.

Down the hall, the logistics staff is burning plenty of the midnight oil, putting together the cargo and passenger manifests. It all has to go—tools, spares, jacks and stands, intake duct covers, tires, LOX converters, test equipment, pencils, files, and, if the deployment is to an austere location, tents, camp stools, cots, coffee urns, and mosquito netting. It's a time for the medical people to get into the act. Shot cards are brought up to date, upcoming annual physicals pulled, cavities filled. A squadron's deployment touches nearly every command on the base. Typically, the move itself is an anticlimax. All the mount-out boxes are loaded onto pallets with weight and volume displayed for the transport crew to check. At some appointed time, the transports (air or surface) arrive, pallets disappear inside, and, in what seems to be no time at all, the cargo and troops are on their way.

Once the squadron aircraft arrive at the destination, the pace of operations jumps into low orbit. Squadrons try to cram the largest amount of training into the smallest amount of time during deployment, and typically they fly almost half-again the number of sorties they were used to back in garrison. There are several reasons for this—the detailed planning that has gone on before, the sensation of being onstage as the new kids on the block, and the fact that away from home there is nothing else to do but work long hours. For the lieutenants, deployment is hog heaven. Collateral duties are usually put on the back burner. It is a time to fly and fly.

Squadron tours vary in length, but in general they are lasting longer—around two years—than they did in the past. With the increasing complexity of the aircraft systems and the missions, it just takes longer to gain an initial proficiency, and longer still to hone those skills to a sharp edge. The best of all situations is the one in which a squadron is "fro-zen"—the personnel roster set in concrete—for an overseas deployment. Members are guaranteed at least two and a half years with the unit, and the squadron enters with a single-minded purpose into a training regimen aimed at reaching the highest stage of readiness by deployment time.

Readiness is the goal from the moment a new pilot hits the squadron. It starts with "putting pegs on the board"—going more or less logically through a set of prescribed flights keyed to the squadron's mission and the aircraft's capabilities. This is what's known as "the syllabus," and completion of the syllabus varies for each aircraft and mission. Broadest of all syllabi is that for the F/A-18, which is logical inasmuch as it is a dual-role aircraft. The F/A-18 syllabus should take a first-tour pilot some eleven to thirteen months to complete, provided such things as carrier deck availability and missile range time fall into place. By contrast, the CH-46 syllabus is less varied, but it takes considerably more time to qualify as helicopter aircraft commander (HAC) because of the additional responsibilities for the safety of passengers that must be assumed by the pilot of a transport aircraft.

Below: Marine Corps A-6 Intruders tied down to carrier flight deck. *Right:* Intruder "over the ramp" en route to arrested carrier landing.

Completing the syllabus is important both as an individual milestone and as a squadron readiness factor, but in a real sense it makes no difference in the day-to-day life of the pilot. He is going to go out and do the same things again and again until they become second nature, and even then, skills like "nap of the earth" flying ("sandblowing") need to be dusted off on a frequent basis. What does change is that as his experience grows, he is liable to find himself cast in the role of instructor for newer arrivals. Proficiency is one thing, whereas excellence is that and a lot more. While both are a matter of repetition and concentration, the latter is a product of mature judgment (termed "headwork" by the initiated) that rarely occurs in one's first tour.

Training takes several forms, varying in the severity of the pressure as well as in the potential consequences to the survival of the individual. At one end of the spectrum are the simulators, in which procedures and techniques are routinized. Simulators, no matter how faithfully they duplicate reality, are not considered substitutes for in-flight training. They are aids to make the real thing more productive, and as this they have made a tremendous difference in the amount of flight time it takes to master a wide range of skills. They are the place to expose and correct bad techniques and ideas, and if they succeed in preventing one accident, they have quite possibly repaid their sizable investment.

On the other end of the training spectrum is actual combat, in which the enormous pressures and physical risks provide on-the-job training opportunities that make all others pale by comparison. Less extreme are the "putting pegs on the board" syllabus flights, special training exercises, and any of a number of highly realistic—and often interservice—adrenaline pumpers such as CAX and Red Flag.

In realistic training, whole squadrons or even air groups or air wings are exercised to simulate combat conditions as closely as possible. It is pointless to have the world's greatest air crews if the planes

are glued to the ground with maintenance and/or supply problems. Likewise, the greatest support doesn't mean squat if the pilot can't hit the target. In routine training, you get chance after chance to do things right, but in combat, you'd better do it right the first time. That's why all the services have developed their own homegrown "wars."

Invariably, the most memorable of all deployments is the one aboard an aircraft carrier. Marine aviators go through periodic carrier qualification training, and from time to time, detachments or even whole squadrons embark for extended periods. It starts with FCLP (field carrier landing practice) sessions, in which the pilots make precision approaches and touchdowns under the guidance of an LSO (landing signal officer) who usually screams pithy invectives into his microphone, referring to such things as lineup, speed, glideslope, and parentage. Nothing is more humbling than a hot summer day with a blustery quartering crosswind. The late-model birds have excellent throttle response compared to their predecessors, but there are still enough "deep-water oogahs" (dives for the deck) and "fly-throughs" (flattening out at the ramp) to keep LSOs from achieving a high complacency quotient.

Aboard ship it's a different world in which time enters a new dimension defined by the heading the ship takes to launch and/or land aircraft. When the carrier turns into the wind something better happen the instant the rudder comes amidships. "In the groove" (on short final to the deck) is not good enough; "at the ramp" is the only acceptable place, and if launches are in progress, one of the catapults better already be in its retract cycle when the first arrival's hook snaps up an arresting wire. From then on, it's "load 'em up and fire for effect" off the cats, and twenty-two second intervals into the arresting gear for returning birds. No sooner will the last launch or recovery have been completed than the ship's helm will go down to establish a new course.

Some leeway is accorded a squadron during its initial qualification sessions, but the grace period is short-lived, particularly in the case of Marines. Being late to man aircraft because the crew can't find the hangar deck—"It's down two flights, cross over to the starboard side and go up three . . ." according to a swabbie who doubles up with glee the minute you're out of sight—is not viewed with great tolerance by an air boss who has just had his ears rattled by an irate skipper. But the Navy/Marine rivalry quickly disappears and soon it's impossible to tell the difference in their performance without reference to the tail letters. Freed from this split-second environment, crew members returning from a tour aboard ship have trouble adjusting to a situation in which the pilot doing his engine run-ups on the runway takes a second look at his instruments before releasing his brakes for takeoff.

It used to be that squadrons would deploy overseas for a thirteen-month unaccompanied (without dependents) tour, but that is no longer the case. These days a deploying squadron makes *split tours* in which it goes out on two separate six-month deployments, spelled in the middle by a sister squadron involved in one end of its own split cycle. The aircraft remain overseas for eighteen months so that each squadron has the opportunity to ferry to and from deployment once during the tour of duty. Upon return home from the second deployment, the squadron is generally "broken up" and reformed with an entirely new complement of officers and men. It's the end of an era, an event marked by nostalgia and sadness.

But there is life for an aviator after the squadron. At the next level up there is the air group, an organization consisting (nominally) of three to five operating squadrons, a higher level aircraft maintenance and repair squadron, a base services squadron, and a headquarters section that provides support for the attached squadrons. Aviators assigned to the group staff fly with the tactical squadrons, maintaining their proficiency as if they belonged to the squadron.

An air wing usually consists of from five to eight groups, and is the basic aviation element in the Marine Corps, which is to say that it is the lowest regularly constituted unit that is self-sufficient. Air groups can be deployed, but they must be augmented by certain wing assets. With the exception of heavy airlift (provided by MAC), a wing can deploy without augmentation from higher command.

There are four wings in the Marine Corps, one for each division. The 1st MAW is headquartered in Japan, 2d MAW at MCAS Cherry Point, North Carolina, and 3d MAW at MCAS El Toro, California. The 4th MAW is made up of reserve units spread around the country and contains some of the most combat-ready units in the Corps, a fact confirmed by the receipt of the "Robert M. Hanson Trophy" for the Corps's outstanding fighter squadron of the year for 1984 by VMFA-112 of the NAS Dallas reserve detachment.

There is a temptation among "reggies" to underestimate the reserves, particularly before the first flight of their annual two-week summer training cruise hosted by the regular establishment. To begin with, they're decidedly "unmilitary." Some have (wow) long hair. They lounge around and giggle and play grab-ass in the ready room, which every-

VMA 311 Skyhawks head home from the Yuma bombing range.

one knows is sacred territory. Often their briefs are cryptic, full of terms and abbreviations such as SOP (standard operating procedures) and "Well, whatever works." But when they're airborne it's a different ball game. There are reserve pilots who are getting more flight time in a week than squadron pilots get in a month. In general, their airplanes are older (though there's a KC-130 squadron getting brand new airplanes straight from the factory), but they are excellently maintained. Even with less sophisticated gear, they are tough to beat on the targets, and when it comes to "fox-ones" and "fox-twos," they give as good as they take.

During his first squadron tour, an aviator may spend 90-percent of his waking hours in squadron-related pursuits, 60 percent of which involves some aspect of flying. During his second tour, these percentages change to 75 and 50 respectively. As a squadron commander, he will go back to the 90-percent figure for squadron involvement, but drop to 30-percent for flying involvement as the administrative demands climb nearly out of sight. The CO (commanding officer) is responsible for every-thing that goes on in his unit whether or not he can directly affect it. This means that he had better be there when his presence can have an influence, especially when safety is involved. And since it is almost impossible to determine which things bear on safety and which don't, you'll find the indelible mark of the Boss on almost everything that goes on.

As the person responsible, the CO of a Marine squadron is the one most in a position to effect safety. It starts with his demands for attention to detail, running from obvious threats such as ignorance, ineptitude, illness, and complacency, to the more remote factors of family problems, poor performance of collateral duties, changing attitudes, and so on. It is not as if the CO doesn't have help in these matters. In addition to his own officers and noncommissioned officers, he can call on the expertise of his squadron's flight surgeon and such outstanding organizations as the Naval Aviation Safety Center. But because it is he who bears the ultimate responsibility for the total performance of his squadron, the CO is the crucial factor.

High-performance military aircraft constitute what is on a daily basis the greatest potential for disaster in our society (although the accident rate in military aviation has exhibited a continuing downward trend). The incredible complexity of the aircraft themselves is a part of the equation, but the real problem lies in the mission, which grows in complexity and risk with each new technological breakthrough. Against these heightened risks, there have been some very real advances in aircraft systems and displays. Solid state circuitry has made a world of difference in both capability and reliability. Test equipment is superb, and maintenance training and procedures even better. Great effort has been expended to make the cockpit workload more manageable, but that in turn has been translated into more capability, not less pressure. Given the realization that there are, and will continue to be, unavoidable accidents, it is the human factor that has affected the decreased accident rate.

Chapter 3
History of Marine Corps Air

On a hot July morning, Sandinista guerrillas mounted an attack on Ocotal, Nicaragua. Outnumbered more than ten-to-one, it appeared that the beleaguered U.S. Marines defending the town could not hold out, but at a little after 10:00, two aircraft appeared overhead. They were Marine fighters on a routine resupply mission and their arrival was coincidence. Sizing up the situation, they began directing machine-gun fire at the attackers, who retreated in disarray. When the planes departed, the rebels remounted the attack. But in mid afternoon, more planes returned to deliver a heavy bombing strike that totally shattered the Sandinistas' battle line. The attack was crushed, leaving dead and wounded strewn at the very edge of the outpost. The remaining attackers fled into the jungle to regroup.

Over the next several months, Marine Air units flew dozens of missions in support of Marine outposts and Nicaraguan troops, keeping the insurgents in check. The climax of the crisis was reached on the next to the last day of December, when the rebels ambushed a Marine ground unit just outside the town of Quilali. Holding a relief column at bay, the guerrillas moved in for the kill. Again, Marine Air came to the rescue, evacuating the wounded and making repeated strikes in coordination with the ground troops. Fighting was to go on sporadically for more than half a year longer, but in the end the Sandinistas were pushed back across the Honduran border. For the first time in several years, free elections could be held in relative peace.

The attack on Ocotal took place in 1927, and it was more than a year before Augusto Sandino and his rebel forces were neutralized. The world has turned over more than once since the DeHavilland DH-4s rained their fury into the steamy Nicaraguan jungles, and it's tempting in the light of current events to ask, "So what else is new?" But surprisingly enough, those turbulent days in that out-of-the-way place marked the beginning of what we know today as close air support. Refined in the Solomons during World War II to meet the coordination requirements of multiunit engagements, the basic techniques developed in the heat of battle went through remarkably few changes until the Korean War, when changes were made primarily because the nature of jet aircraft necessitated greatly increased target acquisition distances. Although Marine Corps aviation had no clear-cut mission until the establishment of the Fleet Marine Force and its amphibious tasking in 1933, those operations in the late twenties and early thirties laid a foundation for Marine Corps air operations that continues to this day.

Naval aviation had been in business for two years before the Marine Corps decided to take the plunge. In May 1912, 1st Lt. Alfred A. Cunningham was ordered to Annapolis, Maryland, where the Navy, with three hydroplanes (two Curtisses and one

Left: Philadelphia, 1911. First Lieutenant Alfred A. Cunningham, the Marine Corps's first pilot, cranks up the "Noisy Man."

DH-4Bs were used against the Sandinistas in Nicaragua in the early twenties.

Wright), had set up a training facility. His first flights were accomplished at Marblehead, Massachusetts, where after something less than three hours flight time he soloed, becoming, as a result, Marine aviator number one—and Naval aviator number four. Shortly, he was joined by Lts. Bernard Smith and William McIlvain, and Marine Air was a going concern.

The first demonstration of aviation capabilities by Marines came in support of fleet operations during exercises held in early 1913 off Cuba. By the end of the year the commandant ordered the establishment of a Marine flying facility at Philadelphia Navy Yard. Meanwhile, the Naval Air Service was created, and the Annapolis training facility was re-

located to Pensacola, Florida. As the move was taking place, Smith and McIlvain joined the Advance Base Brigade in Puerto Rico for the annual Atlantic Fleet exercises, marking the first use of aircraft as an integral part of a Marine expeditionary unit. Despite their success in scouting and reconnaissance operations, the unit was disbanded, and Marine Air once again became part of naval air, where it remained until the declaration of war with the Central Powers in 1917.

When Lieutenant Cunningham organized the

aviation company at Philadelphia Navy Yard in 1917, the number of Marine aviators stood at five, a figure that was to multiply again and again before the end of World War I. Late in the year, a detachment from the unit—now officially designated the 1st Marine Aeronautic Company and flying Curtiss R-6 floatplanes—deployed to Cape May, New Jersey. There it took part in coastal patrol operations in conjunction with its training exercises. Early in 1918, the detachment redeployed to the Azores to participate in antisubmarine operations.

The second and third elements of the company, equipped with land-based aircraft outfitted for service in Europe, found themselves without a mission when the Army refused to have anything to do with them. Cunningham went back to the Navy and argued successfully that his units should be used as part of the antisubmarine force tasked with attacking the Germans at their home bases. Thus was born the Northern Bombing Group, but getting Marine Air into the war was never destined to be simple. The bombing group languished and it took more of recently promoted Captain Cunningham's resourcefulness to (1) take over the Curtiss Flying School in Miami; (2) relocate both elements of his command under one roof in Florida; and (3) recruit aviators away from the Navy to fill his roles of the requisite 135 pilots for the imminent deployment of four squadrons. The first three squadrons embarked for Europe in June 1918, Marine aviation having grown to a strength of 7,500, one fifth of whom were officers.

Their arrival in France in July was a fiasco, and once again Cunningham was put to the test. First, there was no transportation to take his troops the nearly 1,500 kilometers to their base, and then, after he had commandeered a train for the two-day trip, he found that his aircraft had been sent to England by mistake. Most men would have given in to the inevitable, but not zoomie number one. Happily for the Corps, Cunningham was a horse trader of no small accomplishment, and by the time he emerged from negotiations with the British, he had struck a bargain whereby for every three Liberty engines turned over to the British, he would receive a complete DH-4 in return. Moreover, he found that the Royal Air Force (RAF) was aircraft-rich and flight crew-poor, a situation that suited his own needs perfectly. Marine aviators were gratefully received by the British, who did their utmost to expedite their involvement in combat operations.

Because the Germans had abandoned their Atlantic submarine bases, the Northern Bombing Group was out of a mission, allowing these Marine aviators to take part in ground support flights right away. Performing such tasks as reconnaissance, spotting, and resupply, by war's end Marines had flown over fifty missions, shot down four enemy aircraft (against the loss of four Marines), and garnered two medals of honor. Although their participation was a minor footnote when viewed in context of the war itself, the fact that Marine aviators were able to get overseas at all, much less conduct combat operations, was a significant achievement and a tribute to the perseverance of Captain Cunningham and his dedicated followers.

After the war, the fortunes of Marine Air paralleled those of the other services—it found itself pared to barely a thousand men. Cunningham, by then a major, remained at the helm until 1920, when he was replaced by Maj. Thomas C. Turner, who was to remain in charge from 1920 to 1925 and again from 1929 until his untimely death in 1931. During the twenties, the Marine Corps continued to operate its DH-4s (redesignated O2B-1s when Boeing rebuilt several out of metal), acquiring a handful of Thomas-Morse MB-3 Scouts, Vought VE-7 and O2U Corsairs, and Curtiss F6C-1 Hawks. In 1930, the Marines received Boeing F4Bs, which in their variations became the backbone of Marine aviation.

Marine Corps aviation kept busy between the wars, flying and fighting in Central America. Haiti, the Dominican Republic, Nicaragua, and Costa Rica all had problems with guerrilla groups, and in most cases aviation units provided reconnaissance and resupply support. However, as was previously stated, out of these operations grew a crude form of close air support, which was to become synonymous with Marine aviation in the decades to come. More significant in a formal way was the creation of the Fleet Marine Force (FMF), which established as the Corps's mission the seizure of bases for the conduct of naval operations. That occurred in 1933, but it was not until 1939 that the Navy set forth aviation's role: the support of FMF landing operations and replacement for naval carrier squadrons. Be that as it may, the eve of World War II found Marine Air in little better shape than it had been at the cessation of hostilities in 1918—an inferior condition shared by other aviation branches as well.

The first months of the Pacific war were a disaster for U.S. forces, and Marine Air felt the brunt of it. First were the appalling losses at Pearl Harbor. What followed at Wake Island and then at Midway painted an even darker picture. Americans were going into combat in inferior aircraft against a foe whose aviators were seasoned veterans. Of the twenty-five fighters that intercepted the incoming raid at Midway, fifteen were blown out of the sky, and only two remained serviceable after the fight. The bombers fared little better. What success the air units enjoyed was a matter of intrepidity, not preparedness.

Guadalcanal was different. It was the first real test of wills in the Pacific, and Henderson Field became the crux. Had the Japanese not begun an airfield on what was surely the least hospitable island in the Solomons, Guadalcanal would be the same mystery today that it was in July 1942. The mission had little to do with the Solomons. Rabaul, Japan's South Pacific fortress, was the goal, taking up the lion's share of Marine Air attention for more than two years.

The Guadalcanal campaign, which was to last for more than half a year, began in mid July 1942 with the establishment of an airfield 550 miles south at Espiritu Santo in the New Hebrides. Led by General Vandegrift, the 1st Marine Division landed on August 7, the amphibious operation going smoothly. The Japanese garrison was routed, and the Marines turned quickly to finishing the airfield, a feat they accomplished by the 12th with shovels instead of heavy construction equipment. It took until August 20 for the first air units—nineteen fighters and twelve bombers—to arrive. It happened to be the same day the Tenaru River battle began. Nine hundred Japanese, the first in the long succession of replacements smuggled in at night, attacked Marine positions. It was a bitter fight with the Japanese troops charging, falling back, regrouping, and charging again until well into the next day, when the last man died. Marine Air got into the act toward the end, but the day and the glory belonged to the riflemen.

If you were to detail all the worst conditions for aircraft operations, you'd have the Henderson list. When there wasn't engine-choking dust, there was oozing mud—and sometimes both at the same time. There was no refueling or bomb-handling equipment. "Parts supply" was the growing pile of aluminum cadavers that were cannibalized to the bone. There were constant air attacks during the day, and at night, battleships, cruisers, and destroyers pounded the area with their guns. Then there were the insects and leeches, the dysentery and malaria, the lousy food, and no sleep. But mostly there was the realization that the enemy intended to retake the stinking hellhole.

The slugging match with Japanese air began immediately, and though the Cactus Air Force dished out far more than it took, what followed was a war of attrition. Fortunately, the Marines and their guests from the Army and the Navy won it. It had been a very near thing. Going in, our troops were untested, and the enemy was well groomed. Previous experiences showed their air arm's to be more than a match for ours, and much of our equipment was either obsolete or (as in the case of torpedoes) inept. But most importantly, the Japanese Navy, despite its heavy losses at Midway, controlled the sea. Grave as they were, it is probably true that to a certain extent these factors contributed to the enemy's defeat, causing them to assume inferiority where either it didn't exist or where the difference was of little significance. In the overall sense, the Japanese lost the battle for Guadalcanal just as surely as the Americans won it, but of the war in the skies there can be no doubt what the story was. Marine Air in the guise of the Cactus Air Force accomplished an incredible feat, leaving as its legacy, alongside the Marines and soldiers who fought and died for this lousy germ-infested hunk of worthless real estate, names that precipitated the fall from glory of the "Sons of Heaven" — Foss, Carl, Smith, Bauer, Galer, Swett, Sailer, and the list could go on and on. February 8, 1943 marked the end of organized resistance at Guadalcanal, but the implications of the victory ranged far beyond the Solomons. The worst was past. The mystique of Japanese invincibility had been knocked into a coffin, and as 1943 dawned, it was time to nail the lid shut.

A week later, the initial F-4U squadron arrived in the Solomons, and though the first engagement with Rabaul Zeros ended ignominiously with the loss of eleven U.S. aircraft (among which were four F-4Us) against the destruction of only three enemy planes, the handwriting was on the wall. The Marines at last had an airplane that was more than a match for the best the Japanese had. The air war in the Solomons began its lopsided slew. Putting matters into perspective, it must be remembered that the bulk of air activities in the South Pacific was performed by land-based aircraft operated by Army, Navy, Marine, and New Zealand units under the aegis of ComAirSols. Marine Air was merely a cog in the wheel of theater air but, as it turned out, a major one indeed. The significance of Marine Air presence in the South Pacific was not immediately obvious, nor were Marines necessarily the beneficiaries of their own efforts. The U.S. Navy was husbanding its carrier assets, awaiting the arrival of the *Essex* Class vessels and steering well clear of Rabaul in the meantime. In time, emphasis shifted to the Central Pacific, leaving the South Pacific as backwater insofar as the future conduct of the war was concerned. What remained in the Solomons was a war of attrition, and though it may have lacked some of the glamour of the carrier war, it was every bit as important. ComAirSols with Marines in the van succeeded in destroying the cream of Japanese naval air. By the time the swirling air battles of the Marianas took place, the experience level of the Japanese pilots had deteriorated to an unacceptable level.

Backwater or not, amphibious operations continued with U.S. forces moving relentlessly north. In June, Marines came ashore on New Georgia, beginning a campaign that lasted until October, when the Japanese evacuated the bypassed island of Koolombangara. The last invasion in the Solomons took place on Bougainville, the largest island in the chain. The Japanese sent an armada to Rabaul in anticipation of disrupting the landings. The threat was significant enough for Admiral Halsey to send a carrier task group to attack Rabaul in a daring daylight raid. The air strikes so weakened the Japanese fleet that Admiral Kurita had no choice but to retire to Truk. Bougainville's beachhead was secure.

Though attempts at providing close air support had been made at Guadalcanal and at New Georgia, they had proved fruitless. Coordination was the problem, stemming from poor communications. It was determined that artillery could have provided the same service without all the risk and hassle. Still, Marines kept at it, and at Bougainville, CAS finally paid off. Marine bombers worked within seventy-five yards of friendly positions at the battle for "Hellzapoppin Ridge," effectively eliminating resistance from the well-entrenched enemy. Surprisingly, CAS would not figure significantly in Marine ground operations until Peleliu, Iwo Jima, and particularly Okinawa, so the most immediate beneficiaries were Army units in the Philippines.

Rabaul persevered to the end, absorbing nearly 40 million pounds of bombs, one third of which were delivered by Marines, who flew more strikes than the Army, Navy, and United Kingdom units combined. The high point of this operation came in early 1944, when Marines alone were flying an average of nearly a hundred sorties a day. And, when it was decided that several of the atolls in the Marshall group were to be bypassed, the task of applying a daily pounding fell to the Marines. While the repetitive work could hardly have been of great significance, it served to prepare crews for the role they were to play at Okinawa.

Close air support came into its own during the Philippine campaign because for the first time aviation units accepted the fact that theirs was a supporting role, no ifs, ands, or buts. It was a momentous decision, based in great measure on the conclusions of Lt. Col. Keith B. McCutcheon and his staff after poring over records and studies of previous CAS attempts. MAG-24 and MAG-32 were ordered to prepare for CAS operations, and they went at it with a purpose, studying and practicing until they were ready to put the developing doctrine to the acid test. From the slap-dash efforts of Nicaragua and Guadalcanal, through the sophomoric approaches at New Georgia and Bougainville, to the deepening commitment at Peleliu, Marines had forged the weapon. But it was the Navy who took it from the "back of the napkin" stage to the ready room chalkboard level, first at Tarawa, and then in the Marshalls. Even though the CAS wasn't as close as "close" was soon to be-

come, missing out on the action must have been a severe disappointment to the Marine aviators who languished ashore for lack of their own escort carriers. Now they were about to move to the fore.

The curtain rose slowly and uncertainly for CAS in the Philippines, as Army commanders held opinions on the unproven doctrine that ran from skepticism to outright hostility. Few seemed eager to leap into the breach, but once the ball got rolling, the converts grew from a trickle to a torrent, and the word was out. The idea of proceeding without CAS was dead. Marine Air had its act together.

Okinawa was the last battle of the war, and in a way it was a prelude for the Korean conflict five years later. Marine squadrons aboard escort carriers were given the primary task of supporting infantry operations, and made their appearance in what was assumed to be a dress rehearsal for the invasion of Kyushu. In conjunction with their shore-based brethren they were to provide a large share of the air support for Marine and Army infantry units involved in this costliest of all Pacific battles. From the start, the invasion fleet had its hands full

OY-1 flies an artillery control spotting mission over Okinawa, 1945.

January 1943. Grumman F4F Wildcats on the fighter strip at Henderson Field, Guadalcanal.

with kamikaze attacks, the effectiveness of which proved to be far out of proportion to their expenditures of men and material. Had the defenders chosen to oppose the landings, things would have been far worse, and the timetable for wrapping up the war would have lengthened a great deal. Coordination of air strikes was complicated by the configuration of the battlefield, whose sheer breadth precluded on-site control, and in the confusion mistakes were made—but with the corollary that valuable lessons were learned.

The years following the end of World War II saw the introduction of the helicopter and the jet aircraft into the Marine inventory. They also witnessed the near demise of the Corps as the United States disarmed. Although rotary-wing flight had been around for quite some time (the Marine Corps performed a cursory evaluation of the gyrocopter in the mid twenties, finding that it had insufficient payload capacity), World War II spurred the development of the helicopter. But it was untested, complicated, difficult, and obscure—and it suffered from the brutality of its self-induced environment and a host of unresolved physical and mechanical issues that would appear and reappear with each milestone in what has turned out to be the most phenomenal development program in the history of aviation. When the smoke from World War II had cleared, the services began their assessments of lessons learned, and Marines were quick to realize that the traditional means of amphibious warfare had joined the list of casualties at Hiroshima. Though it was Maj. Gen. Roy S. Geiger who stumped for a reevaluation of doctrine and who immediately grasped the helicopter's potential, it was left to the Shepherd Board in 1946 to spell out the aircraft requirements: a 5,000-pound payload to be carried at 100 knots for 200 to 300 nautical miles with an altitude capability of 15,000 feet. Helicopter pioneers Sikorsky and Piasecki concurred in the feasibility of such a design specification, and though it would be nearly ten years before all of the requirements were met, the program proceeded under an austere budget.

HMX-1 was commissioned at Quantico in early 1948 where it exists today. Initially, it operated the HO-3S (Sikorsky) and the HRP (Piasecki), exploring their mission potential in a variety of situations. The first major milestone occurred in May 1949, when sixty-six troops were ferried from the USS *Palau* to Camp Lejeune during Operation Packard II. The fact that with the HRPs grounded it took five HO-3Ss more than twenty sorties to accomplish the mission, did nothing to obscure the essential lesson of the exercise: vertical envelopment was feasible. What remained was the refinement of tactics and the development of new aircraft.

It was becoming increasingly apparent that sweeping changes were in the offing that would affect not merely the utilization of the helicopter in the tactical environment, but the helicopter's potential role in amphibious warfare. It was a momentous time, and in a sense the Corps was staking its existence on these ungainly looking creatures that shuddered and thrashed their way from point A to point B, intent, so it seemed, on clubbing the very atmosphere into submission. They were loud and balky, relying on great gobs of horsepower and tissue-paper thin structures to wrestle minuscule amounts of men and material relatively short distances. If they lived long enough to go through overhaul, the bulk of the machinery was thrown away. To some, they were mavericks, as were the men who flew them. If it can be said that the grim reaper paid more attention to the rotary-wingers than to their fixed-wing brethren, the opposite was true with selection boards. Never mind that the wop-wops were trickier to fly than anything else in the air. Forget that the struggle was not over as long as the rotor blades were still turning. Ignore the fact that the suckers were a compilation of such fundamental inconsistencies that anything short of a perfect landing was likely to end in disaster. It was rough and thankless duty, but the believers hung in there.

Sunday, June 25, 1950 is the date cited as the beginning of the Korean conflict. August 12, 1945, is more accurate, marking the declaration of war by the USSR on the Japanese. Pouring men and material into the northern area, the Russians had all but secured everything north of the thirty-eighth parallel by the time the United States arrived in late September of that year. The crossing of the border in 1950 was a foregone conclusion. The U.S. 24th Infantry Division was called upon to hold the fort while General MacArthur assembled his forces for a counterattack. The 1st Provisional Marine Brigade, consisting of the 5th Marine Regiment and MAG-33, put ashore at Pusan on August 2 and entered the thick of battle on the 7th. Right from the start, Marine helicopters began to show their mettle, carrying supplies, evacuating wounded, spotting for artillery, and carrying out a variety of liaison duties. Marine helicopters entered the Korean War with VMO-6, which operated four different types of aircraft: HO-3S, HO-5S, HTL (Bell), and the OE-1 Birddog. Though the squadron's primary mission was spotting, the choppers involved themselves in an unbelievable variety of operations. Medevac duties were well publicized, but from first to last, VMO-6 acted as a testing ground for chopper ops. The first fully constituted helicopter squadron was HMR-161 which arrived in Korea in August 1951. Operating fifteen HRS-1s, its task was to test the concept of vertical envelopment under battlefield conditions. The test proved to be an immediate success, and throughout the war HMR-161, in concert with its cousin, VMO-6, developed and refined rotary-wing operations.

After a month and a half of gobbling up territory, the North Koreans' advance was stopped and, for a while, reversed, but then they too stiffened, threatening a stalemate on the Pusan Peninsula. It was here that MacArthur dipped into his hat, and

Helicopter evacuates wounded corpsman of the 2d Battalion, Fifth Marines in Korea, 1952.

this time he came up with an assemblage of U.S., British, and Republic of Korea troops to perform one of those "we'll never have them again" amphibious assaults at the mouth of the Inchon harbor. Marines stormed ashore at Wolmi-do, a little island connected to the city by a narrow causeway. It was a daring maneuver for a number of reasons (not the least of which was an adverse tidal situation that allowed infrequent windows for such an assault), but implicit in the success of the operation was the effectiveness of CAS, which was principally the province of Marine Air. By August 17, Kimpo airfield had been secured and three Marine squadrons (two Corsair and one F-7F Tigercat) set up shop.

In the months to come, Marine aviators were to fly more than 2,500 missions in support of ground troops and at the close of operations were to receive enthusiastic congratulations from Army and Marine ground units for their impressive performance. The Marine air/ground team was off and running, and North Korean resistance collapsed in the face of the coordinated attacks. But the real show was yet to come. When the Chinese crossed the Yalu and cut off the Marines, the grunts saddled up, did a one-eighty, and entered into their finest hours. That the glory was theirs is without doubt, but were it not for the air cover that was with them every step of the way, the outcome could well have been different. Meanwhile the Air Force, undaunted by the irrefutable facts, persisted in its denial of CAS doctrine to the very end. Thus the stage was set for Vietnam.

With Korea under its belt, it would be logical to assume that Marine Corps rotary-wing aviation was an established fact, but such was not the case. The Corps was seething with well thought-out challenges to the way that it went about its business, and the Hogaboom Board in 1956 went a long way in spelling them out by affirming that the helicopter was an integral part of the amphibious structure. The problem lay in getting support from the Navy, the Joint Chiefs, and Congress. Things were bad enough for the Army helicopter people, who had the problems of dirt and smoke and gusty winds to make life miserable. How much worse, then, the prospect of operating eggbeaters in the amphibious environment, which added salt spray, pitching decks, long stage lengths often over water, and (because their limited numbers often mandated deployment in small detachments) long distances from maintenance support. Little wonder intra- as well as internecine battles raged. Critics scoffed. Staunch supporters wavered and caved in in the face of seemingly insurmountable problems. A measure before Congress sought to have the Marine Corps role reduced to that of palace guard, and more than one pundit had prewritten the Corps's epitaph.

Nonetheless, the *faithful* persevered, and the years leading up to Vietnam saw the continued development of aircraft and doctrine. By 1962, the Corps could boast of four helicopter air groups equipped with nearly 350 aircraft, two-thirds of which were HUSs (H-34s). During this time, the LPH (landing platform helicopter) came into existence, first with the conversion of the carriers *Thetis Bay, Boxer, Princeton,* and *Valley Forge,* and then with the first of her own class, *Iwo Jima.* Even in the eyes of skeptics, the helicopter was growing up rapidly, making the transition from a battlefield luxury to a down-and-dirty, first-string fighting machine. The H-34 was more rugged and flexible than its predecessors and therefore was a great stride forward, but it was vulnerable and limited when it came to fulfilling the Marine Corps's expectations.

In the same way that the Boeing 707 transformed air transportation overnight from the realm of adventure to ho-hum inevitability, the advent of the turbine helicopter in military aviation revised the order of battle in both the Army and the Marine Corps. Higher speed and payload were part of it, reliability and maintainability another. There was the reduction of vulnerability and a dramatic expansion of the operating envelopes that staggered the imagination of Korea-era pilots, but there was one thing more. Once you get into the helicopter business with both feet, the demand for air crews rapidly exceeds the supply. In the first place, flying helicopters *well* is no snap. In 1962, the eve of the Vietnam War when the boys were waffling along in the piston-pounding H-34s, there were not enough crews to meet the current demand, much less fill future seats. The training time to produce a first-rate wop-wop H-34 driver was just too long. As it was, 1962 was the year of the great "raid the fixed-wing pilot pool" extravaganza in which 500 jet pilots were ordered to transition to helicopters. If this was greeted with discontent in Sleeksville, the helicopter community didn't view it with great enthusiasm either. Many of the fixed-wingers reported in with bad attitudes, and the differences between habit patterns made things worse. What saved the situation from being a disaster was the introduction of turbine-powered helicopters the likes of the UH-1 Bell Huey, CH-46 Boeing Sea Knight, AH-1 Bell Huey Sea Cobra, and CH-53 Sikorsky Sea Stallion.

The decade of the sixties dawned with the Marine Corps still on the defensive when it came to choppers, but then came Vietnam, and all at once it was the Army that had to scramble. Marines had pushed hard developing helicopter tactics and to a certain extent this factor determined the way the war was fought until late in the game, when, with most of the U.S. units withdrawn, North Vietnamese units were able to mass for attack. The tremendous mobility afforded by the helicopter, coupled with the heavy firepower of the tactical jets, prevented the enemy from engaging in large unit actions, and as a result, Marines were able to achieve victory after victory in I-Corps, the northernmost area of South Vietnam, running from Quang Ngai Province to the DMZ.

Despite the variety of procedures and experiments carried out over the nearly ten years of Marine involvement in Vietnam, the one core element was the helicopter. At first, their use was a logical outgrowth of the Korean experience. They moved small units of men and material (often reconnaissance patrols) into remote areas, brought back casualties, provided liaison and intelligence support, and occasionally put down some covering fire. But it didn't stay that way for long. Soon choppers were delivering large numbers of troops and their equipment, taking part in LZ preparation missions, ranging out on low level reconnaissance flights, providing CAS to ground troops, and maintaining a constant flow of men and supplies to and from the battlefield. The air crews lived with the grunts, sharing in their triumphs and losses to an extent that few of the fixed-wingers ever did. As a result, they were generally better able to evaluate and act on the needs of the ground units than were the zoomies.

The H-34 was soon joined (and ultimately replaced) by the Bell UH-1 (slick then gunship), Boeing H-46 troop transport, and Sikorsky CH-53. By 1966, the first of the Bell AH-1 Huey Cobras with their guns and rockets began to make their presence felt in I-Corps, ushering in a new and vital ground support service. The fact is that most targets that pop up during a ground skirmish cannot be seen by the pilots of fixed-wing jets no matter how low they go. It's different in helicopters. Their proximity to the sound and fury of battle gives them a unique vantage point. Even when targets can be marked by ground units or airborne FACs, the uncertainty of the exact locations of the targets and friendly forces as well as routine hang-ups in coordination procedures often conspire to upset the timeliness of fixed-wing air strike support. It is into this niche that helicopters moved so successfully and it was a rare operation that did not involve the support of helicopter gunships.

In the fixed wing arena, in the early stages of the Vietnam War (1965-67), Marine Air operated for the most part in behalf of the grunts. A relatively small proportion of its flights were siphoned

off to strike targets in Laos and North Vietnam; more than 60 percent of launches were directed against preplanned targets in I-Corps. The average elapsed time from the submission of a routine or priority mission request to the time aircraft were on target was slightly less than eight hours during this period. Because the preplanned missions were so successful, hot pad launches comprised a small part of the overall picture. This was fine until the Air Force's reigning "bomb 'em until they quit" philosophy paid off in an ever widening war, necessitating the takeover of Marine Air by the Seventh Air Force. By dint of clever management, the time between the submission of a strike request by a ground commander and when the aircraft got there was reduced to fifty hours. Guess what? The Air Force was right all along. Recognizing the futility of going through conventional channels, Marine ground commanders stopped sending in strike requests for preplanned targets, relying instead on the hot pad to react to situations that had theretofore been handled on the flight schedule. The majority of preplanned targets had little to do with Marine operations. The bulk was used in support of Army units or in punching out tree stands along the Ho Chi Minh Trail.

It was an incredible misuse of Marine tactical air, and for all intents and purposes the Marine air/ground team disappeared. It was one thing trying to support Army units that often lacked the communication equipment and trained personnel to call in strikes. To help them, you had to have an intermediary, but instead of using trained Marine airborne FACs, the Air Force assigned its own crews to the task, and the result was often something less than terrific. The point is that when the Marine air/ground team was allowed to function, it functioned well. Unfortunately, from 1968 on the effort was diluted to the point of only sporadic effectiveness.

The seventies were for Marine Air both an end and a beginning. Driven by criticism from within and without, the Corps began to take a serious look at its assumptions, among them the role of aviation in future wars. Vietnam had been many things to many people, and out of a decade of uncertain action had grown weapons and tactics the use of which will be critiqued, developed, or discarded for years to come. The most important resource was the knowledge and insight of those who had flown in combat, but it wasn't until late in the decade that Marine Air began to evaluate its sacred cows in the light of the Vietnam experience and to make the transition to its modern structure and tactics.

Not all tactics have to do with hostile action. When you're the size of the Marine Corps, you find that it's sometimes easier to fight the enemy than to fend off the good intentions of your friends. The Air Force's attitudes toward close air support are as entrenched as the Corps's; they are almost diametric and are not liable to change to any great extent. While the Navy has "guaranteed" the Corps control over its own aviation units during amphibious operations, it doesn't take a scholar to realize that the very granting of this boon contains the seeds of its refutation should sufficient (in the eyes of the Navy) justification exist. Since Vietnam, the Corps has developed a mix of aircraft and a rationale for their employment that is unique in military aviation. While by no means its founder, the catalyst of this renaissance in Marine aviation has to be Marine Aviation Weapons and Tactics Squadron One (MAWTS-1) of whom more is written elsewhere.

Left: F4B of Marine Fighter Attack Squadron 115 on a bombing run over Vietnam, 1971.

Chapter 4
Main Operating Base

Deteriorating conditions have made it necessary for the United States to send in forces to stabilize the situation. The first step is to establish a master air and logistics base close to the battle area on friendly soil, a Herculean task requiring close coordination with and heavy reliance on the U.S. Air Force's Military Airlift Command. A lot of cargo will come from ships, but envision the streams of C-5s and C-141s that are required to emplace the men and equipment that form a deployed air contingent (in this case an air group consisting of two each F/A-18 Hornet, A-4 Skyhawk, and F-4 Phantom squadrons, one A-6 Intruder squadron, and detachments of four EA-6B Prowlers and twelve KC-130 Hercules), not to mention the tens of thousands of line-item pieces of equipment and consumables that support these aircraft and allow them to perform their missions.

After the main operating base has been established on friendly soil, an amphibious assault is launched sixty miles away against a lightly defended beachhead where Marine infantry, armor, artillery, and support units stage prior to advancing on the major objective, which lies 150 miles inland, 260 miles from the main operating base. Once the beachhead has been secured and a base perimeter established, the off-loading of equipment and supplies commences under protective air cover. Marine fighters operating under fleet air controllers (and perhaps supplemented by Navy fighters as well) maintain air superiority, while attack aircraft conduct strikes against enemy positions and supply routes.

When the foothold is firmly established, the combat elements advance, stretching air and logistic support with each mile. At the point when we take up the action, the ground units have advanced 200 miles north through rolling desert and have reached a mountainous area where the enemy has set up defensive positions. As expected, it is here that a major (and perhaps decisive) battle is shaping up. Though an austere base has been established closer to the FEBA (forward edge of the battle area), the majority of the aviation units still reside at the main base 250 miles southwest of where the action is taking place.

The farther the battlefield is removed from the air base, the more complicated it becomes to provide support for the ground troops. It takes more planes, more sorties, more fuel, and more support facilities and personnel to maintain around-the-clock coverage. Air refueling becomes a way of life; at this distance a tanker must be on station nearly constantly. Where there are tankers, there must be fighters to act as escort, for you have to assume that the enemy knows that without air refuelers your other air capabilities are drastically curtailed. The same is true of your ECM (electronic countermeasures) and ELINT (electronic intelligence) aircraft. With every mile of advance on the ground, the price goes up—and there is a point of no return.

What follows is the development of a coordinated attack aimed at knocking out the enemy's command and control capabilities along with their antiaircraft defense facilities. It is designed to saturate and overwhelm the acquisition and fire control radar systems and, in the midst of the confusion, attack and destroy the launch sites. It is important to keep in mind the fact that nothing guarantees success, and no matter how perfectly the strike is planned and executed, there is still the unexpected. The strike planners take all the intelligence available, digest it, and come up with a mission profile best suited to the situation, but things have a habit of changing. Therefore, the plans must be flexible enough to allow for creative action by the attackers. In battle, particularly during an initial strike at a defended target, you have to be prepared to take losses. If you want to avoid them altogether, you stay home; otherwise you go smoking in there loaded for bear and obliterate the enemy's capabilities the first time around, so that when you come back, he's got nothing left to hit back with. Go get 'em tiger. See you at the debrief.

Dramatis Personae

SCARECROW—black **WAYSIDE**—green **CHARLESTON**—304.5/122.6 FM

CALL SIGN	TYPE	T/O	TOS	IP/OP	TOT	ORD
Panther	EA-6B	0600	0630	Hotel	N/A	ELINT
Brute	2 F4	0600	0630	Hotel	N/A	4D7 8D9
Bat	EA-6B	1800	1840	Lima	N/A	ECM
Hogbody	2 F18	1800	1840	Lima	N/A	8D7 8D9
Volleyball	KC130	1310	1415	Garnet	N/A	20,000 GIVEAWAY
Mad Dog	2 F4	1320	1415	Garnet	N/A	4D7 4D9
Zorch	4 A4	1335	1445	Garnet	1445	CHAFF 4D9 4SHRIKE
Charleston	OA-4	1400	1435	Kilo	Cont	2D9
Sidecar 1&2	EA-6Bs	1400	1425	Delta	Cont	N/A
Whisky	4 F4	1405	1425	Delta	Cont	8D7 8D9
Manta	8 F4	1410	1440	Oscar	1448	96D2 16D7 16D9
Fokker	4 F18	1415	1440	Mike	1446	48D2 8D7 8D9
Longhorn	1 RF4	1425	1450	Tango	1455	PHOTO RECCE
Frog	1 F4	1425	1450	Tango	1455	2D7 2D9
Volleyball	KC130	2215	2315	Hotel	N/A	2315-0515
Skidrow	2 F4	2205	2230	Hotel	0015	24D2 4D9 4D7
Milky 35	A6	2300	2330	Foxtrot	N/A	18D2

*IPs (initial points) and OPs (orbit points) are predetermined reference points over the ground.

Hornet (F/A-18)

There's something preposterous about her. Perhaps it's the way she flaunts her parts in ceaseless and seemingly random abandon. Maybe it's her Buck Rogers styling that makes you doubt her sincerity. She's no brutish Phantom scaring the hell out of you at the very sight. Maybe it's the sense of unreality you get when you see her nose describe an absolutely impossible arc through the sky to bring her weapons to bear, and you realize with total dismay that you've just been eaten alive. But surely the biggest incongruity lies in her name—Hornet. The folks who thought that one up had no vision, no feel for the ages, for if they carried in them the blood lust for combat, they'd have seen in the F/A-18 the stuff of which legends are made. Pegasus for God's sake, not Boxer! Hornets sting. This thing eviscerates. Call her *Rapier* or *Ninja* or *Assassin* or most legitimately *Cobra*. But *Hornet?* Come on, guys.

In January 1984, MAG-11 became the first air group anywhere to be operational with a full bag of F/A-18s. It had been an uphill battle for the airplane, which had begun life as a contender in the Air Force's light weight fighter competition (LWFX). It was 1974, and the two finalists, General Dynamics's YF-16 and Northrop Aviation's YF-17 duked it out over the high desert. Concurrently, the Navy was involved in a search for a highly maneuverable aircraft capable of replacing both the F-4 Phantom and the A-7 Corsair II. Initially there had been proposals advanced by Ling-Temco-Vought, Grumman, and McDonnell Aircraft in addition to those of Northrop and General Dynamics, but because these last two had already produced fly-off prototypes for LWFX, the Navy decided to limit its options to these. The F-16 won the LWFX, but the Navy, evaluating the same data, came to the conclusion that its requirements favored the Northrop entry, providing some major design modifications were incorporated. Northrop, because of its inexperience with carrier suitability requirements, agreed to act as a subcontractor to McDonnell Douglas. The latter, drawing on many of the technological superiorities of its own paper design for VFAX (model 263), began the task of turning the YF-17 Cobra into the F/A-18 Hornet.

VMFA 531's Capt. Tim ''Tiny'' Timm, huge for a fighter jock at 6'3", is still dwarfed by his F/A-18.

The first consideration was to strengthen the fuselage and landing gear for carrier landings and catapult shots, which in turn created the requirement for a larger wing. New weapons systems and radar were added to give the aircraft all-weather weapons capability, and by then it was obvious that the aircraft would have to carry more fuel (nearly twice as much) to meet its mission requirements. When the first Hornet rolled out, its wing area had increased 15 percent and its weight had shot from 23,000 pounds to 35,000 pounds—a whopping 50 percent. To counterbalance the growth, the General Electric F-404 engine (which in its prototype form was designated YJ101 and had powered the YF-17) had completed its extensive testing program with very few teething problems. The low-bypass power plant puts out 16,000 pounds of static thrust, while weighing in at slightly over 2,100 pounds. By contrast, General Electric's J-79 (which powers the F-4, among others) weighs nearly twice as much, is a third again as long, and is mechanically more complex.

Seldom does a flight test program go by without encountering problems, and the Hornet's was no

exception. The landing gear failed on a carrier landing during sea trials, and it was found that stress loads were higher than had been anticipated, necessitating the redesign of the shock strut. Several aerodynamic problems cropped up, but the one that hit the headlines had to do with a less than desirable roll rate in the high transonic (0.95 mach) low-altitude regime. It was shades of the forties—aileron reversal, in which the shock wave makes the aileron act like an antiservo tab. Curing the problem took two steps: (1) strengthening the outboard wing panels; and (2) aerodynamically repositioning

Left: "Star Wars" panel of F/A-18.

Above: Hornet unloads flares to deflect heat-seeking missiles as his wingman's 500-pound bombs rearrange the California desert.

the location of the shock wave through differential movement of the leading edge flaps. Finally, the flight control computer software was tweaked to the point where, with a lateral stick deflection, every single control surface on the airplane does something.

VMFA-314 was the first squadron to make the transition from Phantom to Hornet, taking delivery of its first aircraft in July 1982. By fall, two more squadrons, VMFA-323 and VMFA-531 joined the Black Knights, making MAG-11 the first fully formed F/A-18 air group anywhere. Over the next several years, Hornets will replace the aging F-4 Phantoms, until there are twelve F/A-18 squadrons residing on both coasts and in Hawaii.

So, what makes the Hornet so special? It doesn't go higher, farther, faster, or carry more ordnance than its predecessor the Phantom. It carries the same air-to-air ordnance (Sparrow and Sidewinder missiles) as the Phantom, it costs more, and it doesn't have two seats (except for the trainer). So what's the big deal? The big deal lies in its capabilities, and they're awesome.

At the heart of the matter is the Hornet's tremendous Star Wars system. In the air-to-ground mode, all the pilot does is designate the target in one of a variety of ways, and the electrons do the rest. The key to the Hornet's incredible weapons capability is the Hughes AN/APG-65 radar system, that and the HUD (head up display) and HOTAS (hands on throttle and stick). Together these allow one crewman to do more things than two can in the Phantom. The crucial elements of the system in the ground attack role are long-range surface mapping, air-to-ground ranging to a target that has been designated by the FLIR sensor, the HUD, the LST (laser spot tracker), or from the MFD (multifunction display). Once the pilot has designated the target, the system displays radar and release information on both the HUD and the MFD.

The air-to-air mode is no shabby item either. The system has four separate modes: TWS (track while scan) for air superiority missions, and three ACM modes for use when an adversary is within five nautical miles. The radar is a multimode doppler system with the ability in the TWS mode to find and track as many as ten separate targets at one time, displaying eight on the MFD. Moreover, it

can continue to scan for other targets while locked on to a particular target. But there's more.

In the event of attack by two or more closely spaced aircraft, the system has a raid assessment mode that allows the pilot to pick and choose between or among them. The buzzword here is *sorting*. The first of the ACM modes, called the "boresight" mode, allows the pilot to lock up the opponent by pointing his nose directly at him. The HUD mode searches a twenty-degree horizontal and vertical square, automatically locking up each target it sees. If the pilot rejects the lock, the radar will continue its search until it comes to a new target. The last is the vertical acquisition mode, in which the radar searches a narrow horizontal sector through seventy-four degrees of elevation relative to the aircraft's nose. What this means is that the Hornet pilot has a tremendous advantage going into a dogfight, even against superior odds. Because the system is capable of locking onto a target by itself, and because the HUD allows the pilot to keep his head out of the cockpit at all times and gives him the ability to accept or reject a target or select and fire a missile without once having to take his hands from the throttles and stick, he doesn't have to transition his scan to and from the cockpit—an advantage no other fighter pilot has.

There are other things that aren't quite as obvious, but they mark a radical departure from previous military airplanes. The same systems that provide the pilot with such tremendous air-to-air and air-to-ground weapons capability lessen the cockpit workload under nontactical conditions. The displays and electronic flight systems free the pilot from many tedious chores that most other pilots associate with night and/or all-weather operations. Little things like not having to look into the cockpit to tune radios or navigation gear while holding formation in a thunderstorm. Bigger things like having displays that really show what's going on. But the biggest thing of all has to do with reliability. Unlike its forebears, the Hornet's electronic good-

ies really work, and they are not prone to fail at what always seems to be the worst possible time. The litany goes on.

The terrain avoidance radar permits the plane to penetrate a hostile area at high speed and low altitude, day or night and in any kind of weather, with a high degree of safety; the coupled ACLS (automatic carrier landing system) allows the pilot to make a hands-off approach right to the deck; the aircraft self-checks its systems, removing a large part of the maintenance burden. But enough. Let's go see what it's like to fly one.

You are the wingman on a strike against the enemy's primary staging area in the TAOR (tactical area of responsibility). The area is heavily defended by a variety of antiaircraft systems including SA (surface-to-air)-6, SA-7, and SA-9 missiles as well as radar-controlled 57mm and 85mm guns. This is a joint effort involving four Hornets from your squadron and eight Phantoms from next door, supported by two EA-6Bs with fighter escort, four A-4s carrying chaff dispensers and Shrike antiradiation missiles, and accompanied by a KC-130 tanker and its fighter escort, and an OA-4M TACA

(tactical air control, airborne) aircraft. It is a highly coordinated affair designed to overload the enemy's defenses so completely that they will be rendered useless. At the conclusion of the strike, an RF-4 and escort will overfly the target to assess the damage.

You're dressed and ready, with kneeboard and the duty cup of coffee in hand, slouched in the leatherette seat in the ready-van. It is exactly 0600 when the strike leader who will be aboard the OA-4 begins his brief. Behind him on the blackboard is the lineup for the flights as well as call signs, event times, frequencies, and controlling agencies.

After explaining the purpose of the mission he outlines the general plan for the flight—initial climbout, cruise formations, descent into the target area. Much of this is SOP, so it doesn't need a lot of detail. Mostly you're copying down frequencies and controller call signs. Once the brief has proceeded to the target area, each step comes under the microscope. Altitudes, airspeeds, headings, IPs, timing, separation and attack tactics, specific targets, and egress procedures are singled out and discussed with each flight element leader. After the A-4s run in from the northwest to make a chaff corridor, and while the EA-6s are pounding down the enemy's radar and communications, the Hornets will go after the SAM (surface-to-air missile) sites using a level toss maneuver, followed closely by the Phantoms who are detailed to hit the communications and storage facilities. The total time on target from first to last will be less than five minutes.

After he has covered the return, recovery, emergency, and SAR (search and rescue) portions of the flight, the flight leader turns the brief over to the intelligence officer, who points out the threat both in the target area and during ingress and egress phases. En route, there is the possibility of encountering enemy fighters, which are based 150 miles north of the target. In the event of engagement, the aircraft involved are most likely to be

SU-22s and MiG-23s with aft-quadrant heat-seeking missiles, cannon, and in the case of the latter, forward hemisphere capability with the fast-moving Apex missile. At the target, there are a variety of radars and weapons with which to contend. An earlier EA-6B ELINT flight collected information on enemy emissions in the area, turning over a tape containing raw data to the TERPES (tactical electronic reconnaissance processing and evaluation system . . . whew!) for analysis. The output is an overlay to the contour base map containing information of electronic significance. Using this, the EA-6 crews are able to determine how best to jam enemy radars and broadcast frequencies and advise the strike aircraft on the safest routes in and out of the area.

Next up is the meteorologist, who goes over the winds and weather throughout the route of flight, and after the strike leader recaps the events and settles any points of confusion, the elements split up to discuss specific tactics. As wingman, it's your job to maintain a proper position on the leader, keeping him in sight at all times and calling out tactically significant information (such as "bogey dope"). Again it is stressed that timing is critical. If the A-4s are too early or you're too late, the chaff will have dispersed. If the errors are reversed, there'll be no chaff at all. At the other end, an RF-4 photo bird is due over the target five minutes after your scheduled target time. Each milestone is set out in detail right down to the light-off time, which will occur five minutes earlier than necessary in case there are any aircraft or ordnance problems to be attended to. The extra running time is a penalty, of course, but an acceptable one under the circumstances.

Getting outfitted in flight gear is no simple matter. The basic element is the flightsuit itself, a lightweight brownish green jumper made out of Nomex, a flame-retardant synthetic material. Fastened with zippers and Velcro, it is covered with pockets that are fine for housing things while lounging around the readyroom, but worthless when the rest of the gear is on. The g-suit zips around the middle of your torso and extends all the way down to the ankles. It fits snugly to begin with, but when inflated with engine bleed air supplied by the aircraft g-suit controller, it squeezes tightly to constrict the flow of blood to the lower extremities. This in conjunction with stomach muscle tensing, allows the pilot to experience more than eight gs without blacking out. The torso harness is the outermost garment, a nylon girdle crisscrossed with wide straps whose ends connect to the aircraft's ejection seat. It is meant to hold the pilot firmly in place during maneuvering and to spread the load of parachute opening shock should ejection become necessary. Attached to the torso harness are all kinds of goodies including an inflatable water survival bag, a rescue strobe light, shark repellent, a survival radio, and a helicopter pick-up D-ring. With helmet, oxygen mask, gloves, steel-toed safety shoes, maps, charts, and kneeboard, you've taken on nearly forty pounds of mass—an amount that makes walking around something of a chore, and becomes downright significant when it adds more than 300 pounds to your weight at eight g's. The Hornet was designed to be simple to operate and

Hornet loaded with long-range tanks for cross-country hop.

46

maintain, and this objective has been carried all the way down to the preflight. For once, things are actually easy to check. The truth is that the airplane is fairly capable of checking itself out, a feature that has done wonders in cutting turnaround time. The walk-around is mostly a matter of checking inside several panels, looking over the tires and brakes, inspecting the surfaces for leaks or damage, and checking the rigging of the ejection seat. Even entering the cockpit and strapping in is simple compared to what it is in most fighters, but it's when the electrical power is turned on that the real fun begins. Prestart checks are simple, and unlike the Phantom, the Hornet carries its own starting unit, a small jet engine that not only spools the main engines up to light-off speed, but provides electrical power to the main systems as well.

More time was spent on this plane's cockpit layout than on that of any preceding aircraft, and it shows. About the only goof is the type and location of the timepiece, a leftover from the Crusades called the "eight-day" clock, which is cunningly concealed behind the stick on the lower instrument console. The throttles and stick contain a profusion of switches and buttons, which allow the pilot to keep his hands where they belong for the majority of a flight—particularly where management of the weapons system is concerned. In the matter of displays, the Hornet knows no peer. The MFDs and HUD are terrific, and various displays can be called up with the punch of a finger. Plink, there's a radar map whose raw video signal has been processed and enhanced. Plink again, and there's an attack presentation. A person could go blind plinking around the cockpit and never even leave the chocks. Light-off is swift and eventless, the engines spooling easily up to idle without the hang-ups one sees in a lot of aircraft. In concert with the plane captain, you go through the simple poststart checks following a strict procedure that guarantees that the various control surfaces are cycling to the right place.

"Fokker flight check in."
"Two."
"Three."
"Four." The radio sidetone is crisp and clean.
"Button Two for taxi."
Close the canopy, and even at idle on a hot day the air conditioning unit does its job. You release the brakes, and when the aircraft begins to move, you tap them to make sure they both work. Even with a heavily loaded bird, it takes very little throttle to get moving. You swivel the nose with the rudder pedals, and the aircraft turns. On the taxiway the Hornet wants to get away from you, so you have to pay attention or you'll find yourself speeding.

"Fokker flight cleared for takeoff. Maintain runway heading and contact departure control on three-two five decimal six [325.6 mhz] when safely airborne."

Takeoff will be accomplished by section with thirty-second intervals between elements. Already the other participants in the strike are airborne, proceeding on their assigned routes. Counting yours, the airfield has rocked in the thunderous blast of seventeen jets, and there is another massed strike to follow in less than an hour.

Runup is done on the runway at 80 percent, and after checking the leader's plane and giving him a thumbs-up to show that you're ready, you watch his head bob forward and you're off. The first few seconds of a section takeoff require a lot of jockeying of power on your part as you work to match the leader's setting, but as you approach rotation speed, things settle out. Airborne, the leader gives a winding signal and a head nod indicating gear-up, followed shortly by the flaps-up signal and nod. Transition is hardly noticeable, as the flight control computer makes all the adjustments long before you could begin to respond. Fokker jerks his head back indicating a reduction in power out of the afterburning range, and you transition into the climbout. It's been fifty seconds since brake release, and already you're three miles out at 320 knots, climbing through 2,000 feet. After clearing a low deck of clouds and stabilizing in climb, Fokker signals you to combat spread formation, and the tactical portion of the flight begins.

"Fokker Three and Four are airborne." The leader of the second section confirms the flight's status.

"Roger. Button Black."

Once all aircraft are comfortably airborne, Fokker lead switches the flight to the en route frequency, a change that, like all communications activities, requires the positive acknowledgement of all flight members.

"Two."

"Three."

"Four." There is a pause while the flight switches channels, and then, "Four."

"Three."

"Two."

"Scarecrow [tactical air control center's call sign], Fokker is a flight of four Fox-eighteens airborne with forty-eight Delta-twos, and eight Delta-nines, four Delta-sevens, for mission number one-four-zero, niner-five-golf." Lead is confirming the ordnance load of forty-eight 500-pound bombs, eight Sidewinder and four Sparrow missiles as specified in the frag (mission order). "Roger, Fokker. Sidecar One and Two are estimating point Delta at five-zero. Contact Wayside on Green."

Wayside is the call sign for a Marine air control squadron assigned the task of monitoring all aircraft in the area -hostile or friendly—and providing ground control intercept information to friendly fighters. They will provide information on other aircraft until the flight descends to the attack.

"Roger, Fokker. Wayside reads you loud and clear. Radar contact. I hold your playmates one-zero miles in trail. Sidecar is up this frequency presently at your nine o'clock for thirty miles."

Although this is not considered a high threat area, it is a good idea to keep alert, making occasional jinks in heading and altitude and twisting around to check the area behind and below. Approaching the pushover point, jinking becomes a more serious affair.

"Fokker shifting tactical" alerts Wayside that the flight is going to its attack frequency and is beginning its descent to the low run-in. Until this point, the flight has been proceeding on a northerly heading, but once close to the deck, you wheel eastward and accelerate to 480 knots across the barren wasteland. Though you're still more than five minutes (forty miles) from the IP, it's a good idea to make a thorough check of the switch positions.

Air/ground in the master mode . . . guns position . . . INS (inertial navigation system) with the offset point displayed on the HUD.

Three minutes out, you go to afterburner to kick the speed up to 520 knots and slide out to the leader's starboard (away from the target) side. Indistinct terrain features stream by both sides of the canopy in a kaleidoscope of color and motion. Only the leader's airplane and the IP seem to stand still in the rush. Thirty seconds to go, and there's the IP, a small reddish lava dome with an oversized plug.

One moment the leader is a sharp silhouette against the dun-colored landscape and the next he's a blur, turning from planform to tail-on aspect as he slices away to the north. Delay ten seconds and then—whap! Stick back in your lap holding level at five g's.

Look for your target . . . a cluster of equipment enclosed in earthen berms . . . there they are, just above the canopy bow in your ten o'clock position . . . got them.

Now it's time for the weapons system to strut its stuff. The bombing computer is constantly generating a display of where the bombs will hit at any given instant, and it's your job to guide the airplane to where the pipper will cross the target and then hit the bomb release button at the right time.

The arc of the pipper is a little low . . . drag the pipper up a scooch . . . okay . . . hold it there.

Slow-flying Hornet viewed from open rear cargo door of KC-130 tanker.

The g-suit squeezes tightly around your abdomen and legs as you strain against the pull. The ground below is a frenzy of shapes and colors, the walls of a vortex that lead inevitably to the target. For what seems like an eternity, they are locked there in a world gone mad for its slowness.

The pipper . . . the walls . . . the target.

Then they are one.

Blap! A dozen darts of sinister black trundle from the racks in measured sequence, programmed so that the middle two should impact dead center.

Keep the pull coming . . . don't let her climb.

A pall of dust is already boiling high above as you flash by the pyre what was once the leader's target. The midafternoon sun dazzles your eyes, and you slam the tinted visor down by reflex. You're heading southwest already.

Damn . . . almost overshot the reversal.

Stick hard against the right knee and the Hornet snaps through the upright and spikes its other wingtip on the uneven ground.

Check your six, stupid . . . it's empty . . . keep it jinking.

Operating in the programmed mode, little pods of chaff and dazzling flares burst in your train in what might seem to be a random fashion. It isn't. Their ejections are timed to add to the confusion set up by surprise and ferocity of the attack and the fluttering debris supplied by the A-4s and the sly electronic distortions of the Prowlers' spook gear. Altogether, it's pretty wiggy stuff.

The four strike aircraft streak away from the cloud of dirt, which rises to above 2,000 feet before anviling off to the northeast. A black plume belches skyward, showing the destruction of a fuel storage area by the Phantoms who have arrived on a more northerly heading. As on the in-run, retirement is characterized by high speed at low altitude with nearly continuous random jinks. The INS is able to maintain a fairly accurate calculation of the aircraft's position, but it takes nearly all your concentration to keep from making a hole in the ground. This is where the hours of training pay off. You find that you develop an internal clock that keeps track of the overall flight path in spite of all the jinking. Somehow you just know where you are.

"I've got two bogies twenty left for twelve miles." It's Fokker, who is up ahead at your one o'clock position for half a mile. Sure enough, there are the two radar targets on the HUD closing at better than 900 knots.

"Roger the bogies. You're clear."

"Starboard hard." Fokker is kicking out to a higher angle-off to allow you to establish a proper fighting position as well as to create a more advantageous attack profile should the bogies turn out to be enemy aircraft. The maneuver pushes the bogies to the edge of the scope, and Fokker waits until they're about to drop off before calling for a reversal. Because of the angle-off the closing rate has dropped considerably. Still, in the forty seconds that have elapsed since the first call, the range has dropped to four miles, and there they are, crossing the nose from right to left, silhouetted against a bank of cumulonimbus off to the south. For an instant you struggle to identify them, and then in a flash of recognition, you've got it. They're bandits, SU-22s to be precise.

You fight the temptation to gawk at them, but already you've eased out to line up a shot on the trailing aircraft.

"Fox one." With a belch of fire, a thin dart boils away from beneath Fokker's belly. Almost at once the SUs wheel to the attack. Now you're wings-level head-on to the pair of Fitters as the Sparrow races toward the closer plane.

There's a flash . . . continued closure.

Then the leading bandit's aircraft disintegrates in a rapid succession of pulsing explosions. Now there's the wingman ripping past the wreckage at less than a mile.

Select heat and bring the pipper to the target . . . where's the tone?

A rasping sound fills your headset, confirming that the seeker head of your selected Sidewinder has acquired the infrared signature of the enemy's engine inlet. It seems almost too easy, but you pull the trigger and . . . Whoosh.

"Fox Two." You hear your own voice in the radio's sidetone announcing the launch of the heat-seeking Sidewinder. The five-inch-diameter missile sizzles ahead, appearing to track too low to hit the enemy. Then, when it seems that it must miss, the missile bends into the vertical and collides neatly with the circular intake. As before, there is a pause as if the fates are deciding the outcome by lot, and then a trail of vapor confirms a lethal hit, and even before the cripple flashes by, the canopy blows away followed quickly by ejection seat and pilot. You see all of this and catalog it for the future, but already you're back in search mode checking for other aircraft. The screen is empty, so automatically you bend back around to clear the airspace behind. A stab of panic—you're looking at the business end of a fighter—but as quickly as your adrenaline surges, it wanes as you place Dash Three and Four moving up into supporting position.

"Fokker's clear."

"Roger, turning back starboard to the outbound heading."

Back in the ready room over your second cup of coffee, it will suddenly come to you that it takes longer to tell about it than it did to knock the Fitters into the hereafter.

Intruder (A-6E)

Face it, folks, it's a two-bagger. Not only that, but the guys at Grumman got it all backwards. The blunt end's up front, and the tail is sleeker than an eel—sort of a W. C. Fields stuffed into a mermaid suit. Head on, it looks like a cartoonist's rough of a flying mouse with a worm perched on its nose. Unlike its stablemates it appears to be ponderous and slow, as if it would respond to whip and rein with all the enthusiasm of a basking shark. That looks can be deceiving is generally lost on those who have never flown the bird. Airborne it is quite nimble, and if you load them out equally, sleeker airplanes will actually end up burning more fuel than the A-6 for the same range. It is Grumman Ironworks to the nth degree—along with its cousin the EA-6B, it is the only Bethpage product still in service with the Corps—and that alone should give you pause to reflect on whether something special lurks beneath its dowdy exterior.

The Intruder was introduced to the fleet in 1964, providing the Corps with its first true all-weather attack capability—a talent it was to demonstrate to everyone's satisfaction during the bulk of the Vietnam conflict. *All the World's Aircraft* will tell you that the heart of the system is the IBM AN/ASQ-133 solid-state digital computer, which rides herd on the Norden AN/APQ-154 multimode radar, but they're wrong. There's this thing called a BN (bombardier/navigator) that merits that distinction, but instead of being an assemblage of silicon chips and circuit boards housed in a little black box, it's a collection of neurons and synapses stuffed into a crash helmet. He manipulates all the electronic goodies that allow the Intruder to swoop in low in the dead of night, find a target, destroy it, and make it back before reveille.

The BN sits on the right side, slightly behind and lower than the pilot, facing a panel that is truly intimidating. Displays abound, ringed by switches and rheostats and widgets that all do something—Lord knows what. When it's up and running, the system has so many modes you have to be a Mensa candidate just to name them much less make them work. There is a radar-mapping display that is nearly photographic in its presentation. Cultural features stand out with clarity, making target acquisition possible even at long range. If you get tired of looking at a radar image, how about the FLIR detector? It gives you a TV-like picture of the thermal world, literally turning night into day. There's a mode that lets you acquire a moving target on the ground and another that allows you to offset from a ground beacon. If you want to let the pilot in on what you're seeing, you can't, but you can send information to his VDI (vertical display indicator) for him to follow.

After Grumman's solid F-6F Hellcat and the F-9F Cougar, you thought you knew what "Ironworks" meant. As if to atone for the lithe beauty of the F-11 Tiger, the Grumman folks left no doubt as to the parentage of the Intruder. It is solid stuff, with skin so thick in places you wonder if the Bethpage bruisers were angling for a tank contract as well. You look at the way the wingfold joint is

capped with what looks like a piece of angle iron, and you start to shake your head until you remember that the A-6 is able to get airborne carrying nearly any piece of junk the Corps can find, slung from just about anywhere someone can find a place to hang it, and you decide not to sweat the small stuff.

It takes six minutes from when the engines are fired up for the system to settle down. From the time the present coordinates in latitude, longitude, and elevation are entered into the computer until the aircraft is shut down, the ship's inertial platform keeps track of every little excursion in heading, altitude, and airspeed, summing these into a continuous point in three dimensional space. While it's settling, you're going through your pretaxi checks, while off to your right, the BN is performing a battery of BIT (built-in-test) checks. The first thing you notice about the Intruder's cockpit is that it is huge and, with all the glass of the goldfish bowl canopy, it must have great visibility. The second thing you notice is that the BN's side is sunken and crammed with electronic goodies. He's eyeball-to-eyeball with his console, which projects aft from the dash. The canopy rail hits him at shoulder

In the calm before the storm, a VMA(AW) 224 pilot awaits plane captain's signal to fire up his Intruder.

height, and between the two, he can't see out his side any better than you can. The shock comes when you try looking out your own side. Straight down is great because you sit so high and because the canopy flares outward, allowing you to see beneath the aircraft. To the rear, the shoulder-mounted, slightly tapered wing blocks your view, and as your scan moves forward, a series of canopy bows and windshield mounts combine with indexer boxes, wet compass, and the heavy gunsight to thwart your every effort to see beyond the cockpit's confines. So much for first impressions.

After your flight in the Hornet, takeoff is something less than dramatic, particularly since you are carrying two external wing tanks and eighteen 500-pound bombs. You cob the throttles and wait. The runway lights unlatch and begin a measured march to the rear. The airspeed needle comes off the peg at forty knots and winds inexorably around to lift-off speed. Unlike its swept-wing cousins, which perch for a while before moving smoothly into flight, the Intruder hops from the ground and drills its way to altitude. Gear and flaps sequence up with barely a bobble. The airspeed grinds its way to the 270 mark and you adjust the nose position to hold the speed. For a moment, you're bathed by the reflection of your position lights as you penetrate a low deck of clouds, and then you rip free into the upper air, a pitch-black vault studded with crystalline jewels. Ahead, at the lip of the horizon, perches the waning moon. It is after midnight as you muscle your way into the firmament. A night such as this is one of the unmitigated joys of flying, and it takes a conscious act of will to maintain your concentration on the job at hand.

Instruments normal . . . fuel transfer on . . . let's turn the heat up a bit.

Next to you at arm's length the BN is playing games. He really is. Better than Pac-Man, better than Asteroids, better than all the supertrick two-bit turn-ons at the video parlors, IBM's AN/ASQ-133 computer is the all-time gee-whizzer. The dif-

A VMA 242 A-6 heads for the Chocolate Mountain Target Range with practice bombs on the outboard racks and 500-pound mud-thumpers on the centerline.

ference is that when it's doing its thing, the stakes are for real. Right now he's setting the coordinates and elevation for a simulated target and turning the machine loose. The display on your VDI changes, and a target and steering symbol along with pull-up and release markers appear. Moving downrange at six-and-a-half miles per minute, the benchmarks are quickly behind you, and soon a new attack presentation blossoms before you.

"Wayside, this is Milky Three-Five with eighteen Delta-twos for your control. We're presently on the two-five-five degree radial for forty-two miles at angels [altitude in thousands of feet] one-one."

Ahead, angry thunderstorms guard the TAOR. The weather-guessers were right. The whole area appears to be clobbered, and the moon, which has climbed a quarter of the way up the sky, flirts with the tip of a thunderhead.

"Roger, Milky Three-Five. Orbit Foxtrot at angels one-zero. Remain this frequency."

Foxtrot is an arbitrary point located this side of

the mountains on a 330-degree bearing at fifteen miles from a hastily erected expeditionary radio-navigation facility, so you turn left to a northeasterly heading to intercept the orbit point. Your mission calls for you to stay on station until assigned a target or for forty-five minutes when your relief is scheduled to arrive. This allows you another thirty minutes of screeching around at low altitude before reaching *Bingo* (minimum operational) fuel. At your altitude of 10,000 feet, you are masked from enemy radar by mountains forty miles to the east of Foxtrot reaching as high as 8,000 feet, on whose farther flanks the enemy positions lie.

Even here, orbiting safely in the clear, you can visualize the terrain, though it's shrouded in low-lying scud and pounded by rain. In the last six days you've pored over maps until every minute feature in the TAOR stands out with amazing clarity. Even the grid coordinates of potential targets form in your mind and with them, visions of weaving your way to them in the rugged terrain, blinded by the torrential downpour.

"Milky Three-Five, I've got a FAC with a radar beacon [RABFAC] for you. Contact Mailman One-Four on Gold. He has some movers. Be advised that Black Bat Two-Six [an EA-6B on an ELINT mission] picked up radar emissions in the vicinity of Khirgiz Ridge." That's a bummer. It means that the enemy may have set up a missile site in the TAOR.

"Mailman One-Four, Milky Three-Five at Foxtrot for your control. Standing by to copy mission."

"Roger, Three-Five, from IP Uniform, the target bears zero-three-zero degrees for six decimal two miles. Elevation is twenty-five hundred and fifty feet. It's a slow-moving truck convoy in the hills at the head of the valley. I've got a beacon. There's a friendly recon patrol on the west flank three miles south of the target. Suggest a right pullout and egress on a reciprocal heading."

Your BN has been busy plotting the target location on the map, and an uneasy situation begins to emerge. If an SA-6 site is really there, you'll be within its range. If you go in at minimum altitude—a risky venture at night even in good weather in such rugged terrain—your toss delivery will put you inside its envelope for at least twenty seconds before you can get back low enough for the terrain to hide you from its radar again.

"Beacon to target bearing is zero-eight-six degrees for twenty-four hundred and fifty meters. The beacon is at forty-two hundred and fifty feet elevation. Artillery impacting on the east face of the valley will be lifted for five minutes commencing in one-zero minutes. Suggest a target time in one-two minutes."

The route from Foxtrot to Uniform will take five minutes and from there to the target, with all the maneuvering that will have to be done on the way in will take another three minutes. Already your

BN is simulating the run, putting in the required positional information as well as the planned attack airspeed and heading. The markers show that pull-up will commence three miles short of the target with bomb release occurring a mile later. At twenty degrees pitch, this should put you at 2,500 feet above the ground at the missile's maximum range just as you commence your escape maneuver.

In your mind's eye you see a dimly lit missile fire control radar room watching a phosphorescent *blip* appear on a circular radar console. It pales then blossoms a second and a third time as it is strobed by the revolving antenna trace that shows its measured march toward the center of the screen. Certain now of its track, the operator notifies the launch director, who has already seen the interloper on his console. The in-range warning light appears just as the blip begins to arc away. Then as the distance begins to open, the director hits the launch button, and a sleek dart climbs on a column of blue-white fire and draws off into the stormy night.

You can make it, you tell yourself. As long as the bombs released where the simulation said they would, you can get back out of the radar horizon before the missile can get to you. Once lock-on is broken, the missile will go out of control and self-destruct.

Check weapons switches on and armed . . . one more minute before turning to Uniform . . . okay, start your descent.

Activity in the cockpit begins to accelerate. Already, the top bar is above the horizon line on your VDI, showing that you're approaching terrain at eight miles that is above your altitude (passing 5,000 feet and still descending). Wham! You're into the clouds, and instantly you're slammed sideways in the cockpit and lifted off your seat, forced into your straps as the aircraft falls with a plummeting torrent of air. Thump! Thud! Yaw left. Slew right and drop off on a wing.

Keep on it boobie . . . almost to the deck . . . should see something soon . . . watch the speed!

In all the heaving, the airspeed has bled off twenty knots. Rain is pounding on the canopy, making the terse communications between you and the BN even more difficult than normal. Your workload factor is inching up on 100 percent, and you become even more aware of the interface between your tail and the seat cushion. Uniform is coming up fast, so from here on things are in the critical mode.

The IP was preselected because it sits at the edge of the mountains, right in the mouth of a four-mile-wide corridor leading to the valley containing the target. Here, the ground elevation is 1,500 feet, but with hills and swales, it will follow an upward trend to 2,750 feet at the release point with mammoth hunks of "instant stupid" soaring another 6,000 feet above. No change of mind once you commit. Your only way out is by the same route you take in, unless you want to play games with an SA-6 over its own turf. So as you roll into a right bank at Uniform, you put your life on *hold,* committing unconditionally to the art and ingenuity of a bunch of circuit-burners who at this very instant are probably kicked back over a beer, thinking of the enormous advances that have occurred in electronics since the development of your system.

Inbound to the cleft, you pop out the bottom of the cloud deck, and suddenly you're racing along with your canopy snagging the edge of the scud. It's eerie. Incessant bolts of lightning rip through unseen thunderheads high above. They ricochet off walls of stone, strobing the tumbled earth in a rhythmic frenzy. Jagged boulders snap into bold relief. Cracks and fissures leap out of the void. It's an acid disco gone insane. It's frightening and yet compelling—the ancient lure of the Sirens decked out for break dancing—and you fight the temptation to come off the gauges and work your way to the target visually.

Okay, systems, keep your act together . . . little more to the right . . . no cow pies now, please.

"Milky Three-Five's past Uniform."

"Roger, cleared hot."

Inside the corridor, the buffeting eases and even the raucousness of the lightning mellows. The vertigo you began to experience during the turn from Uniform subsides, and now your mind is focused on the mission at hand. You're rocketing along as if blindfolded, knowing full well that at less than two miles on either side there are banks of cumulo-granite—the hardest clouds known to man. What keeps you out of them is your preconception of the terrain, confirmed by the computer-generated presentation of radar data before you on the VDI. When it can see that far (it can't now because it's staring at the hills beyond the dogleg, which are now at five miles), it will scan eight to ten miles ahead of the aircraft, providing a stylized presentation of the terrain fifteen degrees on either side of the aircraft's flight path. As long as the elevation bars in front of the aircraft are below the horizon bar, you'll clear the ground. Just how far ahead you need to

alter the aircraft's flight path depends on the ruggedness of the terrain and on your desire to get the total and unwavering attention of your BN. For level to slightly rolling countryside, you can guts it down to the second elevation bar, but here, the third is better because there are excursions of from 300 to 500 feet within the corridor. The dogleg is coming up rapidly.

Roll her up and bring her around to 010 degrees . . . don't climb . . . oh, hell . . . cow pies!

At this speed, you have to really honk the aircraft around to keep the turn radius down—sixty degrees bank angle and two g's —and the terrain avoidance radar system can't hack it. Sensing the rapid turn, it responds by shutting itself down, recognizing that its presentation is ancient history. What you see on the VDI is a bunch of ovals, or cow pies (squares on late model stuff), which is its way of saying, You're on your own, Ace.

"Sweet beacon." Your BN has acquired the beacon signal, authenticated it with a special code, and loaded the target information into the system.

That's trust and confidence for you. You're groping your way through the mung, blind, and your BN is busy minding his store. The *computer-to-attack* light blinks on, and the target symbol and steering presentation with pull-up and release markers pop up on your VDI. The computer has generated the offset points from the beacon, providing you with tracking information on both the VDI and the HUD. Were it not for the clouds, the BN could try to acquire the target with the FLIR and designate the target more precisely, but in this case it is going to be beacon all the way to release.

In the right seat, the BN is going crazy flipping back and forth between search radar and beacon mode. It is important for him to keep oriented just in case your system crashes or you need help. You listen to the rasp of rapid breathing in the ICS (intercommunications system), and you realize that you're both knocking down oxygen at a furious rate.

At times like this, your thoughts are elliptical; they pulse like staccato daggers. In setting them down they seem random, even vague, but in reality they are highly structured, fashioned into a powerful tool over years of taking the senses to the outer edge of their limits.

There's the valley . . . come right to 030 . . . oops, don't go low . . . get on the steering line.

Ka-bump! The aircraft lifts abruptly in a sharp-edged gust and falls out beneath you, but by this time you've got a thirty-psi lip-lock on the seat pan that would take minus ten g's to break. The rain begins to beat down even harder than before, and without thinking you push the throttles up to the stops to raise your speed for the weapons run. The release maneuver is a loft, in which the aircraft is rotated with a four-g pull following the steering line until the tracking solution is satisfied and the bombs are released. You don't have to begin the loft right at the computed pull-up point—you could wait until you're right on top of the target and then perform what is known as an "over the shoulder" loft in which you release the bomb going pretty much straight up—but in this case you want to remain as far away from the target as possible, which accounts for your desire to get as much airspeed as you can. The faster you go, the farther out from the target you'll be at release, and as if to echo your thoughts, the "pull-up" and "release" markers move outward on the courseline.

Commit trigger . . . master arm on . . . get ready.

In a flash of cognition, you see the whole thing, charging along at nearly 450 knots, 500 feet above a climbing valley floor, struggling to keep the courseline where it belongs. Crouched on the hillside against the clubbing wind and rain, the FAC hears you rush past, and he strains to make out the bomb hits in the midst of the tempest. Somewhere to the north, a radar operator is about to get the shock of his life when you materialize out of nowhere, and three miles ahead, unbeknownst to their drivers, a bunch of trucks are about to rendezvous with 9,000 pounds of high explosive.

At the pull up . . . four thousand feet . . . another thousand to go . . . come on you mother, get there.

There is an eternity crammed into that nanosecond just before the bombs kick free, during which everything seems to go into a hold mode. It's like the weapons system trainer put into the "freeze" position. You have this crazy sensation that there's time to go to the head, grab a Coke, and when you get back, it will all still be there just the way you left it.

The bombs have no sooner begun to trundle from the racks than the RAW (radar acquisition warning) system goes "able sugar." It is simultaneous, as if they are linked events. With a lit RAW scope, and a pre-set 140-milliseconds delay between the release of the individual bombs coming off the racks you find that you can count every single one of those hummers. The final thud hasn't even translated from the rack to your seat and you've already reefed the bird into a 120-degree bank to the right and hauled the stick into your lap. Cow pies again, along with grunts in the ICS. Behind the aircraft bundles of chaff and brilliant flares go off to mark your passage.

One-eight-zero . . . two-zero-zero . . . roll out.

The ground is coming up quickly and you break the descent rate from 3,000 feet per minute to 1,500, then 750, leveling off at 3,400 feet—500 feet above the ground. The VDI sorts itself out again and you're converging on the outbound track. If the missile hasn't found you by now, it never will, because back down low, you're out of its controlling radar's line of sight.

"You've got secondary explosions, Milky," advises the FAC, confirming the accuracy of the drop. "Way to go!"

Later, en route to home base, you turn to your BN, who is still playing games with the system, and offer up the duty catch-all.

"Piece of cake."

"Roger that."

Prowler (EA-6B)

Without a doubt it's its parents' child—a combination W. C. Fields and Mae West—but somehow it came out looking prettier. Maybe it's because the cockpit extension makes it more comely, or perhaps it's because over the years we've become accustomed to the homeliness of the Intruder. Whatever, the EA-6B is a "keeper" and that's good because, like the Good Fairy, when it waves its magic wand it confers the cloak of invisibility on a lot of good guys who need it.

VMAQ-2 is the only squadron in the Corps operating the Prowler. Replacing the hastily cluged together EA-6A, the four-place B-model is an honest-to-goodness "go out and rip their lips off" ECM platform, able to launch from ship or runway into the ravages of hell itself, listen for the softest heartbeats in the electronic spectrum, reduce to mewling trash the probing fingers of enemy inquisition, and return with a detailed bit-map of their electronic order of battle.

The keys are things with the improbable names of ECMO and TERPES. (No, they're not part of puberty, and you don't get them in hot tubs.) In the Navy you can have one and not the other, but in the Marines they are inextricably linked. Elec-

Above: Transmitter pod is wheeled into position for centerline installation on a VMAQ 2 Prowler.

Right: Prowler engine bay dwarfs mechanic. Engine is the powerful Pratt & Whitney J-52-P-408.

tronic countermeasures officers are the folks who fill three of the four seats in the Prowler, and the tactical electronic reconnaissance processing and evaluation system is what they come home to. As a slight concession to the overpopulated aviator community, Grumman saved one seat for a pilot, but the fact remains that the EA-6 is the ECMO's bailiwick. For all the cosmetic differences, the Prowler is essentially an A-6 with a second row of seats, a bulge on the tail, more powerful engines, and a little added beef in some of its critical parts to put up with its increased weight. The distinction is not in what it is, but what it does.

It is not true that if you've seen one ECMO you've seen them all—they speciate right there in public. The one in the front cockpit is basically the "pilot control officer," managing the communications, navigation, defensive ECM systems, and when time permits, he jams enemy communications. He also provides lookout for the right side of the aircraft. The ECMOs in the back are the skulduggers, and to do their black deeds, they connive, dividing up the threat bands as you would a pizza. The receiving antennae are located in the tail, segmented to determine the direction from which a signal is

coming. The ECMOs select the frequency ranges in which they are interested, divvying them up to ease the workload. When a radiation in a designated band comes on, a logo appears on the screen, defining the emitter's true bearing from the aircraft as well as its frequency. The ECMO may then elect to engage it with an appropriate jammer carried in any of five pods slung beneath the aircraft. Each jammer is for a certain frequency band—there are eight spectra—and if you don't happen to have the proper band aboard (or if it is already engaged) you're out of luck.

Electronic warfare is as much a game of stealth as it is of frequency clobbering, and a lot of it is cat and mouse. Whether the specific mission is active or passive, a recording is being made of every single item of electronic significance that takes place during the flight. Airborne, the ECMOs are busy working their displays, so often the "big picture" eludes them. But back on the ground it is a different matter, and that's where TERPES comes in. At the end of a flight, the data tape is fed into a computer. The precise aircraft position, altitude, and heading throughout the flight and the true bearing and frequency of perceived radiations are input. From these, TERPES creates an electronic map overlay that details the location and (inferentially) the type of electronic gear that's out there. Everything from radar sweeps to Navaid transmissions is there, and when you throw in the time sequence, the electronic order of battle emerges.

Armed with the latest information on the location and types of enemy gear, the ECMO is able to select the proper jammers and lay out a flight profile to engage and defeat them. He can also enter into the aircraft's system coordinates and pertinent data that allow it to ease his in-flight workload. This way, instead of responding to threats, the system is actively out there looking for particular signals, poised to jump on them if and when they appear.

Systems are nice and they can do a lot without the assistance or interference of man, but the truth is that ECM is still a black art whose high priests are the ECMOs. There are general rules and ranges of probabilities, but in electronic warfare there are no givens. What works one time does not always work another. You can't just tell the system to blast old Scheisskopf over there and go back to the Sunday crossword. Some things require the finesse of a Houdini, and that's where you separate the true magicians from the mortals. To be a good ECMO you need to be clever. To be a great one you must be diabolical.

An ELINT mission actually begins long before the flight itself back in the TERPES complex, a hovel comprised of three Dempster Dumpsters pushed together to form a U. Here it happens to stand out from most of the other similar tactical spaces because it's painted in jungle camouflage instead of desert dun, so you don't have to worry about walking into someone else's refrigerated office. As your eyes adjust to the dim light, you see that both consoles are occupied, and the Hewlett-Packard pen-plotter is going crazy printing out an overlay. On the wall there's a 1:250,000 map that includes the area of concern, while on the drafting table there's a 1:50,000 map of the TAOR. The plotter ends its absurd jerkings and the TERPES officer removes the overlay and, after a careful matching of the line-up marks, he tapes it in place on the table. What you've got is the real world, spattered with electronic pecker tracks. It's "all we know about the enemy's radar and radio capability," but it's nearly twenty-four hours old, so it's time to go out and do some more snooping, and it's your job to design the flight profile for a pre-strike passive electronic support measures mission.

You lay out the route to check enemy capabilities in different sectors and at various altitudes, searching for gaps and weaknesses in their coverage. Do their radars have frequency-shifting capability? If so, is it random? Is there a pattern? What is their response time? These and a hundred other questions need to be considered before you cut your tape to preprogram the aircraft's system, and then it's time for the brief. You're assigned to fly in the fourth seat, right side aft, and it will be your job to monitor for air-to-air radar emissions as well as those associated with antiaircraft artillery fire control. Your left seat companion will

concentrate on acquisition and SAM fire control radar frequencies, and the front seat ECMO will monitor radio transmissions while helping the pilot maintain the preplanned profile exactly. Even though each ECMO is concerned with his own slice of the action, it is a team effort. If one of the displays goes down, the remaining console will have to carry the full load.

The mission is an entity unto itself, and to carry it out there will be two fighters flying escort, but there is an overriding purpose beyond the generalized collection of electronic data: to accurately assess the enemy's ability to detect and engage a coordinated raid against his vital area scheduled for later in the day, and in so doing, arrive at a plan of attack to defeat him.

It's still dark as you walk out to the airplane and begin to strap in. Just getting aboard in all your gear is a chore by itself, and you never lose your fear of falling off the boarding steps or slipping from the rain-slick canopy rail. There's a cutaway in the dash panel that allows you to view the pilot as he and the front-seat ECMO work through the prestart checks. Presently, the port engine turns over, spun by impingement air from a smaller jet engine mounted in a mobile start cart. Though you can't see the instruments that confirm light-off, you can feel it through the light vibration in the airframe. Slowly at first, and then more rapidly as it approaches idle, the engine spools to life, and then the pilot switches to internal electrical power. There is more to the start sequence, but it's time for you to get busy setting up the system

The heart of the EA-6B is the ALQ-99 advanced ECM central processor, which is accessed through either or both rear seat consoles and consists of a screen, an input panel, and several function select buttons. Selecting signal frequencies agreed upon during the brief is essentially a matter of telling the system to reject others. You set in 9,000 to 9,500 mhz for air-to-air radar and 2,700 through 2,900 mhz to capture the AAA (antiaircraft artillery) fire

Above: Rear-seat ECMOs feed data into ALQ-99 computer prior to Prowler mission.

Below: Loaded with ECM pods and long-range tanks a VMAQ 2 Prowler departs Cherry Point on cross-country flight to Nellis AFB, Nevada.

Above: Fin bulge contains Prowler's radar receiving antennas.

Below: VMAQ 2 pilot and trio of ECMO "wizards" pose with their immense EA-6B at Cherry Point.

control stuff, and the numbers appear on the left side of the display. Similarly, by establishing the true azimuth of interest, you are saying, in essence, Look here and ignore that. As you proceed with the route you will be constantly changing the true bearing, but for the time, you select the sixty-degree cone from 010 to 070, and the numbers are displayed at the top of the screen. Latitudes and longitudes of previously plotted emitters are already in the computer's memory. They and their capabilities have already been analyzed; it's the new things and the changes that matter, particularly when you consider how mobile some of the new Soviet antiaircraft defenses are.

When at last you look up, the final poststart checks are being performed, and the plane captain, now visible in the soft gray light, relays the "pull chocks" signal to his assistants crouching beneath the wings. The pilot adds power to get under way, taps the brakes sharply to confirm their stopping authority, causing the nose to dip, and rolls smartly toward the taxiway. Ahead, the pair of Phantoms, wing and fuselage lights winking cheerfully against the growing dawn, are headed for the arming area, where their missiles' pigtails will be plugged in and safing pins removed. The pilot and the forward ECMO are still working challenge and response against a seemingly endless checklist, and at last all that remains are the runups on the runway.

Prior to taking the runway, only the pilot and the forward ECMO have been on "hot mike" over the ICS, but now that the aircraft is ready for flight, all four crewmen are on the loop, a fact confirmed by the increased sound of breathing. It's not that anyone is panting, but the depth and rapidity of breathing goes up for things like takeoffs and landings, and with four people in on the act, you notice it.

The engines are run up individually and their pressures and temperatures checked. Outside there is a huge racket that is being heard for miles, but in the cockpit the sound is rather pleasant, wrapping itself around the breathing and the muted ring of the electrical system as it plays through the ICS. Satisfied that all is well in the bowels of the ship, the pilot advances the throttles to an intermediate position, takes his feet off the brakes, and advances to takeoff power. Initially you're aware that you've rocked back into the seat, but with every second the Prowler is gathering momentum and soon the runway lights are tearing past at a furious pace. Without jammer pods, this thing is a goer. The nose lifts, the wheels unstick, and you dance into the air . . . just like that.

At 5,000 feet, the morning air is smooth as glass. The first spike of sunlight, piercing yellow in the moistureless air, stabs through the Plexiglas side-window, lighting it with an ethereal glow as millions of tiny scratches give birth to microscopic rainbows. It's entrancing and you find with a start that your eyes are focused at six inches instead of at infinity, where they should be, in the performance of your lookout responsibilities.

"Want to become an ace?" you heard at your first multistrike briefing for crews of the fighters and EA-6s. "Escort the ECM birds, and I promise you'll get a look at a lot of MiGs." It's true. The Prowler is a ripe plum; that's why it is escorted in combat. But that isn't to say that it's meat on the table. With its big wing and hot-rodded engines, it can turn and manage energy with most anyone. It doesn't have any offensive missile capability, and it shouldn't have. Only fighters should fight fighters, but the EA-6 can turn until it drives a fighter to a high angle-off and then run like hell in the other direction. With fighter escort, a Prowler should be able to hold an attacker at bay long enough to allow time for a friendly fighter to settle Ivan's hash.

Because of the relatively low altitude, your selected frequency band search, and the narrow field of view, the video display remains empty for the first 200 miles. Then the first phosphorescent stutters appear, followed magically by the blossoming of a symbol near the center of the screen. Unlike a radar blip, whose location is a reflection of the target's direction and distance relative to the receiving antenna, this mark lies at the intersection of the source's true bearing (somewhere between 010 and 070 across the horizontal axis) and its frequency (between 2,700 and 2,900 mhz on the vertical axis). From its present location you can tell that this radar is in the AAA (antiaircraft artillery) fire control frequency range (a suspicion confirmed by the computer's analysis and signaled by the assignment of the symbol "A") and that it lies somewhere along a line 040 degrees from the aircraft's present position. The computer assigns a variety of characters depending on what it knows in the first place. In this case it is saying that this is a 57mm gun-laying radar located at such-and-such a location. It says this because it has been programmed to look for this particular radar at a particular spot. What it sees is that the right signal is coming from the right direction, but it could be another radar that happens to be lying on the same line when the system first saw it. If this were the case, as you continue to move, the computer would notice that the expected bearing for the known radar and for this one were diverging, and at some point it would acknowledge the fact by canceling the "A" and assigning a new symbol.

Because this mission is passive, you have relatively little to do; the real work begins back at the TERPES when the flight data tape gets processed. But later this afternoon when you're going in loaded for bear with wall-to-wall jamming pods, you'll be flipping back and forth between displays in a frenzy, assigning jammers to the applicable emitters as they come into view. Armed with prior information, a lot of the work can be preplanned, but there's always the unexpected. Sure, the work is hard and nerve-racking, but the pay's good and there's a lot of solace in knowing that because your wits have picked up a new threat and dealt with it effectively, some "attack puke" will be able to squirt unseen through a hole in the electronic curtain.

Homeward bound with the screen empty again you think for a minute about the guy at the other end of this deal—a toad sitting out there looking at his radar scope, knowing you're out there somewhere doing something to him—or about to do something to him. What does he think about? Is he trying to negate that little edge you're trying to give the attacker? Does he have an ace up his sleeve? And finally you think about the upcoming strike mission and you wonder whether Ivan has something up his sleeve you don't know about. And for an instant you fall prey to the ancient fear of all practitioners of the occult: What if my powers fail me?

Above: Prowler ECM transmitter pods are quickly interchangeable. Nose propellers drive generators for internal electrical power.

Skyhawk (A-4M, OA-4M)

There's an immense ripping sound overhead, and a tiny dart flashes by, pulling streamers from triangular stubs as it heaves quickly up and around in a pop-up double-roll dive delivery maneuver. One moment, its silhouette is fixed against the uncertain backdrop, and then as if by some cosmic sleight of hand, the A-4M in its "no see 'em" paint scheme of gray-blues disappears into the void. Only the noise remains, filling the sky from wall to wall with a shrill cacophony of varying sounds.

Tying yourself to the A-4M Skyhawk is a little like putting on suspenders. It's an airplane that you buckle *on,* not *into.* Your hands and feet are swallowed up in the cramped confines of switches, le-

vers, and displays that give the pilot dominion over the Corps's smallest fixed-wing tactical jet, a distinction the Scooter has borne since its introduction to the fleet nearly three decades ago. The Skyhawk is another—and arguably the best—in a long list of superior aircraft that have sprung from the fertile mind of Douglas Aircraft's long-time design genius, E. H. Heinemann. Construction of the first prototype began in September 1953. The first flight came in June 1954, and when the production line was finally closed in February 1979, nearly three thousand A-4s (A-4A to A-4N) had entered service. Significantly, the last plane off the line was an A-4M destined for the Marine Corps, and while plans call for AV-8Bs to replace the last A4-Ms on active duty in 1992, don't place any bets on it.

Initially it was built as a lightweight, reliable, and cheap jet replacement for the aging AD (A-1) Skyraider that was capable of nuclear weapons delivery. If that had been where it stopped, it would long since have ceased to exist. But beyond the excellence of the design, the very features that allowed it to lug what was then a heavy and clumsy weapon also let it carry an enormous load of conventional weapons. For all the changes that have been incorporated over the years, the design philosophy itself has never changed. This is a tribute first and foremost to the Navy and Marine Corps planners, generations of whom have known a good thing when they've seen it.

Right from the start, the Skyhawk was subjected to refinements and modifications that allowed it to fill new roles and respond to the changing combat environment. A refueling probe and hydraulically powered control surfaces marked the first major revision. The addition of radar, more weapons stations, and an eventual engine change came in orderly succession. In the ensuing years, there has hardly been a piece of air-to-ground ordnance that has not found itself slung beneath the little screamer, and lest the fighter community think itself pristine, Marine Skyhawks were configured for Sidewinders in the early sixties and stationed aboard ASW (antisubmarine warfare) carriers to provide air-to-air support.

The A-4M was designed specifically for the Marine Corps, incorporating the lessons learned by U.S. and Israeli pilots over the years. Small as it is, the enlarged goldfish bowl canopy allows nearly 360-degree visibility, a far cry from the earlier variants. Unlike its intermediate predecessors, the A-4M has no radar, restricting its primary mission to the daylight VFR (visual flight rules) regime. The entire upper avionics bay—the humpback that first appeared on A-4Es during the Vietnam War—is

crammed with ECM gear. Fully loaded, the A-4 weighs less than an empty Phantom and its head-on radar cross section is less than a third of that of its illustrious cousin. In many respects it comes closer to its earliest ancestors than those that came in between, particularly from the standpoint of being a hot rod. In a sense it is the super-Skyhawk with a thrust-to-weight ratio that in some circumstances approaches that of fighter planes. The Pratt and Whitney J-52-P-408 puts out 11,200 pounds of static thrust, increasing not only its climb and sustained maneuverability performance, but its low-level dash capability as well.

The five hardpoints underneath the aircraft allow it to carry a wide mixture of air-to-ground and air-to-air ordnance externally, while retaining guns ca-

pability with two internally housed 20mm cannons in the wing roots. The nose contains a pilot-slewable TV camera adapted from the "Walleye" camera-guided smart bomb, whose image is projected on a screen on the left side of the dashboard. The boresight point of the TV camera is projected onto the pilot's HUD, and it is this or the laser spot tracker that allows him to designate the target to the ARBS (angle rate bombing system). Once the target has been designated by the pilot, the ARBS integrates information supplied by the aircraft's angle of attack and barostatic sensors with the rate of change in target bearing to solve the tracking problem. The HUD presents the pilot with steering information and determines the correct point of release. This allows the pilot to fly a random flight path to the target instead of a preplanned wings-level glide that increases his exposure. The accuracy of the system is phenomenal compared to manual bombing. How does ARBS compare with the more sophisticated system found in the F/A-18? It is not as accurate, though the difference is not all that great, and negligible when a high degree of contrast between the target and the surrounding area exists. One factor weighs heavily on the side of ARBS—it is passive. It cannot be spoofed or jammed, nor does it provide a signature that would attract antiaircraft devices.

That the Skyhawk remains in the Marine Corps inventory is a matter of controversy. That it is a VFR-only attack plane in an era in which many of the missions are flown at night or in foul weather is a typical challenge, and not without merit. Another is, How can you afford a single-mission aircraft when the cost of engines and airframes is so expensive? Yet there is another side of the argument—one advanced with some authority by the Israelis and the Argentinians, whose opponents would be somewhat less quick to dismiss the Skyhawk's potential even in this era of super sophistication. Light, nimble, quick, rugged, reliable, hard to spot—these are the Scooter's more obvious at-

tributes, and they are not without significance when you're duking it out over unfriendly territory while operating in an austere and perhaps inhospitable expeditionary environment. Time and again, circumstances have arisen to give the Skyhawk a new lease on life. Why then is the Corps so eager to phase it out?

It's not an easy question to answer. At the staff level there seems to be a fair consensus that it's time to move on to a new basic attack plane. "We need something that is not tied to your conventional airfield at all" is a common argument advanced by tactical proponents of the AV-8 program. "Every time we get around the Air Force, Marine Air becomes another little part of theater air" is another familiar lament. "If we station the AV-8s with the forward ground elements, maybe the on-scene commander can count on Marine CAS." They are good points, and they have taken the day in terms of procurement. A-4s will be replaced by AV-8Bs as quickly as the latter can be produced, and there will be no attempt to upgrade the Skyhawk's capabilities.

"Look," begins a third-tour Skyhawk pilot/WTI whose intensity tells you that this is no lightweight matter to him. "When you analyze the threats that are out there and our ability to accomplish our mission, there is no single school solution. From the standpoint of the pilot, he has to work his way into the area, position the aircraft to acquire and designate the target, maneuver to deliver the weaponry, and finally get the hell out of there—all without getting dinged. The small frontal area makes it about the hardest aircraft for the enemy to pick out on radar, and this gives us a shade of an advantage going into the target area."

There are other things as well. "You take the maintenance hours per flight hour; the cost of equipping, staffing, and maintaining a twelve-plane squadron, not to mention the investment in the birds themselves, and the Skyhawk stands out as a bargain." This isn't to detract from the capabilities of the other aircraft, but to point out the obvious that for some roles, the A-4M is still a winner.

Finally, there is that special feeling that A-4 pilots share, a sense of purpose and a special pride that comes with the VFR attack mission. There is something so real and immediate about zorching around in the weeds in your Mark-One Mod-Zero tinkertoy that fanaticism flourishes—and there's room for lots of that when the serious shooting starts.

The primary variant of the basic Skyhawk is the OA-4M. It's a thinly disguised TA-4F, like the kind students use to frighten flight instructors in the Training Command. So what's it doing flying over the battlefield? "It's just a gimmick to get the staff guys some flight time," is a semitypical quip heard around squadron ready rooms. A lot of the flak comes from the fact that the OA-4 is not *really* an M-model in the sense that it still uses the Pratt and Whitney J-52-P-8 engine instead of the more powerful P-408 version that fills the single-seater's belly, yet at the same time it is heavier and exhibits more drag in the clean configuration than its TA-4F progenitor. Compared to either the A-4M or the TA-4F, it's a dog, but so are a lot of other airplanes—it's the mission that makes the difference.

Like the OV-10, it's a case in which the Marine Corps has taken an existing aircraft and adapted it to fill a badly needed role. The OA-4M is a TACA two-seated, "this way to the war, guys" aircraft, sprouting radios and antennae all over the place. It's a "fast" FAC whose value comes to the fore when the air defenses make things just too hot for the OV-10s. Operating at 450 knots, it doesn't give away much maneuverability, so it's hardly what you could call a sitting duck. What is interesting is that while the need obviously exists (as it did in Vietnam, where aging F-9 Cougars were pressed into service) there is no other aircraft in the U.S. inventory to fill the role—which explains its perennial participation in joint exercises such as Red Flag at Nellis AFB. What it gives the Corps is an edge in a high-threat area where terrain is a factor

in communications. It would be nice if ground stations could communicate with all aircraft at all times, but it isn't possible, even if their transmitters were located on the top of Mount Everest. Time after time, the Vietnam experience showed the need for airborne air control, even if it was merely a matter of relaying information up and down.

OA-4s are found in the H&MS (headquarters and maintenance squadron) units, and they are usually flown by group staff pilots, but it's not like the old days when air groups kept several trainer aircraft around for proficiency flying. The OA-4 pilots are school-trained FACs, and a large percentage of them are MAWTS-1 graduates. Often, they are called upon to brief and coordinate multiaircraft strikes, particularly if a high degree of flexibility is called for.

But enough of this, it's time to get the show on the road. You'll be first on target, hardly a comforting thought, but one you've come to live with. If they know you're coming, there'll be lots of that stuff that goes pop and fizz even in the daytime. Still, there are some things on your side. You're small, hard to spot, nimble, and what's more important, you're not radiating anything in the way of electrons and little of IR (infrared) significance. Most of all, you know the *when, where,* and *what* of your mission and they don't, and that gives you the edge.

Your job is to go bustering into the target area to lay down chaff to confuse the enemy radar. It doesn't seem like much—just hanging a bunch of tinfoil out to flutter in the breeze—but if it succeeds in creating even a slight amount of indecision, the other aircraft will achieve surprise as well.

The plan is for you to head nearly due north and rendezvous with a refueling tanker eighty miles short of Garnet, a control point at the edge of the TAOR which is your pushover point. After taking on 2,500 pounds of fuel apiece, you'll turn east from Garnet and descend down to the deck, arcing around to enter the target area from the north—an unexpected direction, and one masked by a range of mountains—until the final dash-in. If you are acquired by radar, you'll launch Shrike antiradiation missiles to home on the signal, so even if you lose the element of surprise, you are not totally helpless.

It's no big deal, you say. Just a two-hour flight from takeoff to landing during which time you and your wingman will climb to 5,000 feet, cruise out 150 miles to catch up with a KC-130 tanker, plug into a bouncing basket, detach and descend to low altitude, penetrate hostile airspace, dash to the target at under 300 feet, deliver the chaff and Shrike, retire at high speed, climb to 27,000 feet, and finally return to base. Piece of cake, right?

The mission begins long before you sign out the aircraft. First, the chaff and Shrikes have to be ordered, then the firing circuitry tested for continuity. Bundles of chaff are then loaded into their receptacles, and finally, after the aircraft are fired up, additional chaff is stuffed into the speedbrake wells and the doors closed to hold it in. It means

you'll have no speedbrakes to slow down to tanker speed, but the extra junk is worth the effort. There are roughly forty hours of maintenance associated with one hour of flight time, so you don't go about the mission in a cavalier manner. In a typical evolution, flight line crews and ordnancemen swarm over the aircraft as it returns from its previous mission. The bird is refueled, its systems serviced and replenished, tires and brakes checked, racks stripped of spent release cartridges and reloaded according to the demands of the schedule, guns recharged and ammunition replaced. If there are any squawks, the appropriate shop or shops order out the necessary parts and proceed to replace or repair the offending items. Sometimes a part is not in ready supply, which means pilfering it from another aircraft or, perhaps that its own gizzards will get raided to ready other birds for flight. Engines—the same as used in the EA-6Bs—are critical items, particularly since Prowlers have priority for spares.

The two-seat OA-4M variant offers high-speed battlefield observation capability. Bird carries extra air-to-ground radio systems in rear cockpit.

While ordnance and maintenance crews do their jobs, you and your wingmen are upstairs studying the maps and mission data in preparation for working out your plan of attack. Once the background matters are over, you begin your mission planning in earnest, because on this flight you will traverse more than 650 nautical miles of real estate, a third of which will be flown at high speed and very low altitude—the most demanding of all flight regimes. Weather, winds at altitude, temperature, probability of contrail formation, intelligence on enemy antiaircraft defenses, SAR (search and rescue) information, escape and evasion, IFF squawks, authentication codes, safe return corridors—these and dozens of other arcane matters must be addressed before you're ready to hoof it out to the aircraft. Although theirs is a supporting role, both the pilot and the copilot of the tanker as well as the crews of their fighter escort have participated in the entire brief. It will be the tanker's job to get you to the right spot over the ground and release you with an accurate position update. Because his climb and cruise characteristics are so different, he will precede you airborne by twenty minutes and you and your wingmen will make a running rendezvous 150 miles up range.

Besides the chaff and Shrikes, you're carrying a pair of 300-gallon drop tanks on the inboard wing stations. Internally you've got 400 rounds of ammunition to feed the pair of 20mm cannons buried in the wing roots. What with the flare and chaff dispensing panels, turtleback crammed to the walls with ECM gear, chin-mounted TV camera, and the wild assortment of antennae bristling here and there, this Scooter is a busy little guy. Now at last you can go earn some of those flight skins (flight pay).

With the relatively light load, flying the Scooter is a ball. You cob the throttle and barrel down the runway until the incredibly tiny wings start sucking on enough air to lever it off the ground. The nose pitches slightly with gear retraction, and there is just the slightest settling sensation when the flaps

"Tom Cats" A-4 lugs 1,000-pound laser-guided bomb on left pylon.

come up. Sometimes you get a bobble if one of the aerodynamic slats on the leading edge of each wing comes up sooner than the other, but mostly it is a delight usually reserved for the afterburner contingent, with the 5,000-foot level-off coming almost before you have time to think about it.

During the early part of the flight you are able to validate your location over the ground with information from navaids, but before you've gone fifty miles from the field, they are out of range. From there on you are dependent on your own preflight planning for precise positioning. So far, you've been flying in combat spread formation, your wingman positioned a mile west, abeam and slightly stepped down, while the second section is deployed two miles east with the wingman farthest away stepped up. Thus arrayed, each flight member is able to view the airspace behind the rest of the flight and provide mutual support in the event of attack. Though you've maintained radio silence since initial check-in, you're monitoring Wayside's frequency in the event he picks up an incoming raid.

OA-4 gasses up from KC-130 tanker off the California coast. Unlike their Air Force brethren, Marine Corps and Navy aircraft are configured to do the plug-in.

Twenty minutes after takeoff you spot the tanker, ahead and a mile to the left. Giving an exaggerated wing drop, you signal the flight to join on you and reducing power to slow to tanker speed (200 knots), you begin your slide to arrive off the tanker's left wing to observe the drogue deployment. The nylon basket, two feet in diameter, slides into the airstream, dragging its eighty-foot hose to its fully extended position. An amber light on the back of the pod confirms that the system is ready. Checking your fuel management panel to make sure you're in the external position, you leave your wingman on the left drogue and cross under to line up behind the right basket.

After stabilizing the refueling probe ten feet aft and slightly below the drogue, you add power to create a five to seven-foot-per-minute rate of closure. The key to plugging in is smoothness, but even then there is no guarantee that you will get an engagement every time. Despite the probe's exaggerated right step, the airflow in front of its tip is disturbed, causing the basket to dance during the final stage of the approach. The trick is to keep out

of a fencing match; you want to make sure that you have a high enough rate of closure to get through the disruption area as quickly as possible, yet not so quickly that if you miss you'll overrun the drogue and damage it or your aircraft. Once contact is made, the probe tip drives into a locking collar and mates snugly, but before fuel transfer begins, you have to drive the hose forward a minimum of two feet. As fuel begins to flow, there is one small danger. If the connection is not complete, fuel can escape and become ingested by the intake, causing the aircraft to autoaccelerate or (gulp) explode, but luckily you live right, so all you have to do is hang on and fly precise formation for the three to four minutes it will take to get your fuel. As the green light on the back of the pod winks off, signaling the end of transfer, you check your gauges to confirm that you've gotten your full amount before reducing power to disengage. Dropping back, you pick up your wingman and pass the lead to your section leader and watch as his flight moves into position and plugs. When they finish, you slide down and away to the right, clearing the tanker well to the east before turning to resume course.

Garnet is an artificial point over the ground, but it also happens to correspond to a series of three conical hills that form the vertices of an equilateral triangle whose altitude is almost directly along the route of flight. Thus, it is not only easy to spot from this altitude, but virtually unmistakable. Wheeling eastward over it, you commence descent by allowing the nose to fall through to a ten-degree dive and once the speed has built up to 480 knots, you reduce the power to maintain a 1,000-foot-per-minute rate of descent. As you roll out on the new heading, you motion the flight back out to combat spread, though at low altitude there is no step-up or step-down.

Even with the HUD, staying oriented with one another while navigating to the target is a handful. At 480 knots you're gobbling up nearly three football fields a second, and at 250 feet above the ground the horizon is less than two minutes ahead. A flat object such as a road may be in your field of vision for less than five seconds, if indeed it isn't masked by vegetation. If you wait to see landmarks and then orient yourself, you'll get lost. You have to anticipate what's coming up and let the landmarks validate your position. There's another caveat. If you let your attention wander for just an instant, you yourself can become a landmark of sorts—let the nose drop ten degrees, and you're into the ground in two seconds. If you have to spend a lot of your time studying your map, you've got a problem. Though less obvious, fatigue is another factor. Bounding along over undulating terrain and alternating vegetation on a hot day is a real thrill. You're being thrown around the cockpit with the violence of an off-road race, your helmet splatting off both sides of the canopy and your shins barking the rudder tunnels as your feet come off the pedals. Sometimes you can tune yourself to the gyrations, but mostly it's a grit-your-teeth, "remember how much fun you're having" affair.

For the first fifty miles you're over barren desert carved with ancient rills and punctuated by wind-eroded volcanic mounds. Punch out here and not even the jackals will mess with your bones before the next ice age. The wasteland doesn't terminate all at once, but gradually you find yourself dodging through rising terrain until you're actually in the mountains. The flight has dropped back into trail, clinging to you desperately as you wheel through narrow passes. Swathes of green-studded granite flow past in a continuum of instant death. No time to look at the map now—keeping oriented while juking through canyons whose walls are continually within scant seconds puts you into that ominous regime of 115-percent sensory overload.

Magically you burst clear of the labyrinth and into a broad, undulating valley. Dash Two slides out to the right and aft along a forty-five-degree bearing line while the second section moves out to the right, abeam. Ahead, in the distant wall, is a deep notch clothed in green and to the right, atop

Skyhawk departs Yuma with tiny practice bombs on multiple ejector racks.

the highest hill, a radar site, one of several you're here to spoof. It's uncanny, but it's just as you envisioned it from the first. You're two and a half minutes from the start of the chaff line.

Check Shrike in Needles mode . . . Master Arm on . . . keep it down in the bushes.

Bing. The ECM threat indicator lights off like a Christmas tree. The needles on the ADI (attitude director instrument) are sitting high and to the right. You've been found by radar. You feel tiny needles dancing on your scalp as your adrenaline level rises, but inside the wheelhouse, the cognitive process is proceeding under fine control. Instead of being a "gimme," you've got some muscle of your own.

Push station five button . . . chaff in program mode . . . hang in there, guy . . . now!

Fire-walling the throttle and thumbing the chaff button on the catapult grip, you roll sixty degrees starboard and haul in backstick, bringing the nose thirty-five degrees skyward. The altimeter wants to self-destruct as the needle winds clockwise at the speed of heat. The number 3 appears in the altimeter window as the needles quiver and snap to the center—lock-on—and you hit the bomb "pickle," triggering the Shrike, which sizzles away to the east. Even before burnout, you've continued your roll to the right twenty degrees past inverted and pulled the nose well below the horizon, slewing the plane forty degrees north of the attack heading. As the wings come level, you check your tail for company and continue the march. Back at low altitude, all your attention is focused on the attack itself—missiles or no, it's out of your hands from now on, and though you sense it rather than see it, Dash Two has closed to your eight o'clock position for 300 feet while Three and Four have fallen into a stepped-out quarter mile trail in anticipation of the delivery.

At some point, you've felt yourself become aloof from the frenetic activities in the cockpit. It could be adrenaline, or it could be that you've done it all before. Or maybe there is something so heady in this area of ultimate risk that you are able to transfer out into an automatic mode. Your hands and feet and eyes are going at full tilt—or faster—yet for you there is a zone of quiet and order in which the chaos and confusion of the moment are held in check.

The run itself is nothing, merely a set of markers in a block of eternity. Press the chaff and hope you don't get zapped while you're flying along straight and level like a fat turkey. When the dispensers have emptied, toggle the speedbrakes open and closed again and wait until the others have done the same. You feel every single nanosecond. You feel yourself marking time at half-step, and the thought is one of unending agony. You can count the leaves on every branch that stutters by in that frame-by-frame slow motion that has neither beginning nor end. The distance to the hills is interminable, and then there is the cleft in the rock, and you excrete out into the valley beyond like a cork from a bottle. In the transition there is just the slightest sense of giddiness, and then there is the escape.

During the planning stage, there is the temptation to let up on the return portion, but to do so is an error that old/bold pilots never make. Your first consideration is to get out of the immediate area as quickly as possible, using terrain to mask yourself from eyeballs and radar. Essentially, the closer you are to the flanks of the hills, the harder it is for anyone to spot you. Your flight plan calls for you to turn south, staying on the eastern slope of the hills for two minutes until you come to a gap where you can turn southwest and eventually west to the desert and thence home. It isn't written anywhere, but you ought to save your highest energy level for this segment of the mission, performing two jinks for every one during the leg inbound. True, you've accomplished your primary mission, but the element of surprise is lost, and though it would be more punitive than tactically significant, getting bagged on the way home is no less painful. Ten minutes after leaving the target—eighty miles to the southwest—it should be safe to commence a climb to 27,000 feet for the cruise back to the base. There, you can begin to wind down . . . but not much.

Phantom II (F-4J/S RF-4B)

Look as you will, there's nothing to trace the F-4's lineage to the sleek beauties that had filled the sky since the dawn of the jet age. Incredibly clean and lovingly sculpted, Russia's and America's contributions to the fringes of space seemed more in keeping with the Louvre than with the battle-field. Only the British seemed to know how to make brutish looking airplanes. But somewhere in the bowels of McDonnell Aircraft, there were Philis-tines, heretics whispering, "It's the mission that counts, let aesthetics take care of themselves," and the world of aircraft design has never quite gotten over the result. Mean and nasty looking in the chocks, it's even more menacing in flight. "Dou-

ble ugly" doesn't begin to describe the brute when it's loaded for bear with racks and rails and bombs and missiles. It has all the refinement of a battering ram with wings, and like no plane before or since, it's easy to visualize the Phantom "punching a hole in the sky." But it's at its best dirtied up for land-ing, looking for all the world like a raptor in search of prey. Between ear-rending screams from the boundary layer control, the Phantom howls and moans with demonic fury. For others, landings are arrivals, but the Phantom's is an event. Wings curled hawklike, head high, its tire-taloned gear reach for the deck. Wham! The engines give a final shriek as the wheels slam down trailing a stream of burn-ing rubber to mark the kill. The chute snakes back, bobs for a moment in the visible wake, and snags

Trailing shafts of molten gore against a glowing Yuma sunset, a VMFAT 101 student enters irretrievably the world of the Marine Corps fighter pilot.

73

Phantom of VMFAT 101 heads toward fog-enshrouded California coast for some real-life instrument flying.

the air with a pop. Her head bows in the firm deceleration, and what remains is a terrible silence.

As with its replacement, the F/A-18, the first Marine squadron to receive the Phantom II was VMFA-314 (then designated VMF(AW)-314), only this was back in May of 1961. Surprisingly, the Phantom was originally designed as an attack plane, but it ended up as a finalist against LTV's F-8U-3 and Douglas' F-5D in the Navy's all-weather fighter modernization program. The F-8U-1 and -2 were already in service with both the Navy and Marine Corps, but neither version had all-weather capability. The winner was to replace the Douglas F-4D Skyray. All three were impressive airplanes, but in the end, the Phantom's twin-engine two-seat configuration held the day. The first flight of the F-4H-1 took place in November 1957, but by the time that the aircraft reached the fleet in 1961, the airplane had been modified to the extent that production aircraft were redesignated F-4H-2 or, as it is now known, the F-4B.

It was an immediate winner, exhibiting capabilities that were an order of magnitude greater than anything that had come before it. Speed and time-to-climb records tumbled on an almost daily basis. As fleet experience accumulated, pilots found that the F-4B could do a broader range of missions than anyone could have imagined at the outset. Initially conceived as the key to fleet defense, its radar reached more than twice as far as the F-4D's. The all-aspect Sparrow missile could be fired at a target long before it could be visually acquired. Its high thrust-to-weight ratio made it a formidable dog fighter, and its powerful stability augmentation system allowed it to excel in the air-to-ground mode as well. It is capable of mach 2 at altitude, and yet it comes aboard ship like a pussycat, providing the pilot with a greater degree of glideslope control than any previous jet. Its pair of General Electric J-79s gave it 34,000 pounds of static thrust in afterburner, and its large fuel capacity and air refueling capability allowed it to range long distances to carry the battle to enemy soil.

It was a tremendous accomplishment. No production airplane in history exhibited a range of performance close to the Phantom's—roughly ten times the speed differential from approach (125 knots) to high-altitude dash (1,300 knots). Adaptability was its hallmark from the outset, not only in terms of mission capability, but being able to grow into the realities of an ever changing threat environment as well. Unlike most of its predecessors and contemporaries, the "manta ray with earmuffs" was able to incorporate new gear without losing out in performance. Moreover, advances in aerodynamics and metallurgy have actually improved its maneuverability and safety in its latest configurations. There was a time when you really had to watch what you were doing when the airspeed decayed toward zero. After departure from normal flight (a memorable event christened the "Phantom thing"), the monster had a tendency to flatten out into an unrecoverable spin. Now, with the addition of leading edge maneuvering flaps, you can point the nose straight into the vertical and leave it there—and live to talk about it. This same feature lets you honk the aircraft around very quickly at low speed, allowing you to bring its weapons to bear far more quickly than you could with its predecessors. As you might suspect, capabilities like these are not without a price tag. The late model F-4 has less stability about its pitch axis, which in turn limits the amount and location of air-to-ground stores it can carry, a fair trade if you consider that the next air-to-air environment might not be as permissive as the one we found in Vietnam.

F-4 of VMFA 451 from MCAS Beaufort, South Carolina, overnights at Yuma en route to Kaneohe, Hawaii.

While acknowledging the contributions of the other fine planes that shared the load there (F-105, A-4, A-7, and A-6 to name just a few), the Phantom II was the premier tactical aircraft of the Vietnam War, and the fact that Marines employed it almost exclusively in the air-to-ground regime does not detract from its value as a multipurpose aircraft. The Phantom will be in the Marine Corps inventory—albeit with the reserves—for many years to come.

Before we launch on a fighter mission, we ought to talk for a moment about a continuing superiority of the Phantom—its recce version. There's an axiom in bridge that "one peek is worth two finesses"—a harmless reminder that knowing what's going on in your neighbor's backyard is a powerful tool indeed. On the battlefield it's the same, except you're not talking about a little snooping at a tenth of a cent per point, but about the potential for the loss of thousands of troops. Governments pour incredible amounts of their treasuries into knowing what's going on in the world around them. At the top of the pile are espionage and "national technical means" (a euphemism for a variety of sophisticated remote eavesdropping techniques), which provide the high-level planners with a wealth of

On a West Coast deployment, ordnancemen from VMFA 451 load 500-pound "slick" bombs on inboard triple-ejector rack.

information on enemy activities and intents. In the next tier are electronic information-gathering and processing methods and high-altitude aerial reconnaissance, which fill in more gaps. The tactical value of such information lies not so much in its accuracy and/or resolution (though these are considerations), but in the timeliness of its dissemination. The Tweedledees and Tweedledums in Washington can gloat all they want over their splendidly acquired knowledge, but if the on-site commander doesn't have it in time to do something with it, it's tactically worthless—of historical interest, perhaps, but an impediment to sound judgment.

In the Civil War, a gent named James Lowell pioneered the use of observation balloons for keeping track of the ebb and flow of battle, often drawing maps and pictures and tossing them to the people on the ground. It was not as precise as persuading Matthew Brady to take his camera up in the gondola, but it was a harbinger of things to come. The combination of airplane and camera came of age during the First World War, and purists will point out that pursuit planes—immediate ancestors of fighters—were developed to "pursue" reconnaissance planes whose valuable information constituted a constant threat. In terms of materials, a lot has changed since those days. There are incredible films, sensitive to spectra well outside the human optic range, and cameras whose lenses can record a license plate number from miles away. To the extent that they are ill-suited to any other task, the planes are specialized too, designed not to blast their way in and out of the target area, but to get in and out before the enemy has time to react. For twenty years, the undisputed king of the tactical reconnaissance hill has been the RF-4, and though the Air Force's C-model has some additional capabilities that boggle the mind (such as digitally processed data transmitted in real time), the RF-4B in the hands of Marine recce pilots remains the battlefield commander's most up-to-the-minute and reliable source of information (other than that sup-

Above: RF-4B of VMFP 3, El Toro, taxies in trailing drage chute.

Below: Each of them decked out in forty pounds of fashionable attire, a two-man crew from VMFP 3 prepares to mount up.

Above: Marine RF-4s remain saddled with smoky J-79 engines, although F-4 fighter-bombers have been re-engined with smokeless version.

Below: All Marine ground crews drill periodically in cumbersome chemical warfare gear, often for many sweaty hours at a stretch.

plied by on-site recce teams, whose coverage is highly localized).

"What's the big deal with the recce pukes?" the typical fighter pilot questions as he contorts his arms into impossible pretzels to demonstrate how he just set up a "kill." "They don't get into delta-mach or pinces or fox-ones or any of the neat stuff. They just fly along in a straight line for five minutes and go home, right?" Wrong.

True, you'll rarely find a photo guy (front- or back-seater) playing "there I was" with his hands, but it's probably because he can think of better ways to employ them. If you stop to consider it, aviation is the school on relative motion, with combat flying being the postgrad course. For the fighter pilot, the job is a matter of maneuvering one aircraft against another in a vast arena of air, a difficult and demanding task but one that can be mastered by men still in the prime of their lives. For the recce pilot, much as for the attack puke, the arena is dirt, but unlike the guy with a raft of bombs, his is not a single spot but a line of points, which means that his margin for error is small. You can come ripping in, two, three, even ten degrees off your planned bombing heading, and make up for it during the final maneuvering. Not so in a photo run; a minor difference in track can throw the whole run off. It's not just that you could miss spotting a target. You could bring back the most wonderful photographs of the juiciest target that ever lived, but if your track wasn't where it was supposed to be, your flight will have been a waste. With so small a margin for error, it's no wonder the recce folks exhibit an attention to detail that is singular among aviators.

The first thing you appreciate on the walk-around inspection is that the Phantom is a large bird with lots of features to catch your attention. Each of the wheel wells contains a variety of accumulator and emergency air pressure gauges that must be checked prior to flight. The underside of the fuselage is an obstacle course, with racks, rails, pylons, external fuel tanks, and ordnance slung all over the place. Sparrow missiles fit into recesses designed specially for them, but the rest of the external stores, along with gear and auxiliary air doors, speed brakes, and trailing edge flaps (which occasionally bleed down between flights) seem cunningly placed to inflict painful damage to the crew member during preflight. In all, there are nearly a hundred individual items to be checked before you are ready to crawl into the cockpit.

As in most high-performance aircraft, strap-in is no cinch. Before anything else, oxygen, communications, anti-g-suit lines, and helmet-mounted sight have to be connected and checked. Next, you buckle on leg-restraint garters, making sure the lines that attach to the cockpit floor are not fouled. If you have to eject, the lines draw your legs back against the seat, preventing them from being guillotined by the dash panel. Finally, you tie yourself to the plane by attaching four fittings to their corresponding D-rings on your torso harness, and after you've snugged the straps up, you're ready to proceed with the prestart checks.

Prior to applying electrical power, you've got to check or position nearly a hundred switches while your RIO is going through his list. There are no shortcuts; a mispositioned switch can cause aircraft damage or even (as in the case of the armament safety override switch) death and destruction. It's an item-by-item affair that guards against complacency. Until you select external power, it pays to take your time to ensure that everything is set up properly to begin with, because afterward the pace accelerates and builds inexorably until you're back home and in the chocks again.

With external power applied, the cockpit comes to life. Gyros shimmy and writhe, erecting in a frenzy of activity. Dials snap off their pegs, climbing to their prestart readings. The telelight panel displays conditions and/or positions of various systems, and with press-to-test buttons, you check the continuity of warning circuits and indicators. After

a bit, things settle down and you're ready to start engines.

Although you've gone through your final brief separately, your flight section's mission is to escort a KC-130 as it refuels a flight of A-4s en route to their target and then proceeds to an orbit station in case returning aircraft require additional fuel to get home. The truth of tactical aviation is that the farther the battle area is from where the aircraft are based, the more critical the fuel situation, the more aircraft needed to run the mission, and the more difficult the command and control problem.

From the instant you bring the throttles out of the cut-off position, the clock is running, in more ways than one. In the time it will take for you to light off, run through ground checks, taxi, arm, and perform your runups, you will have burned 350 pounds of fuel, an amount equal to that required to fly thirty miles or more in the air. During takeoff and acceleration to climb speed, you will boil off another 725 pounds, and by the time you level off at 7,500 feet and run the tanker down, you will have consumed nearly one tenth of the original 22,000 pounds you started with—full internal fuel (12,900) pounds) plus two 370-gallon external wing tanks and one 600-gallon centerline tank (9,100 pounds)—and you still have another 130 nautical miles to go before you reach the A-4 refueling point. Every little deviation from the planned mission costs you fuel—the indispensable element of flight. If you light off too soon, you'll burn an extra amount because of the increased running time. If you light off late or get delayed for any reason, you'll have to increase your cruise speed by going to a higher power setting. Once on station, you're at the mercy of circumstances. The Skyhawks might be late, or you may have to intercept a raid. You may even have to engage in a fight requiring extensive use of afterburner, and for this you pay dearest of all. At intermediate altitudes, you will burn something in the neighborhood of a thousand pounds of fuel per minute in afterburner, and when you consider that when all is said and done you still have roughly 150 miles to get home from the tanker orbit point (1,200 pounds of fuel at optimum altitude using an idle descent to landing), you can see that the pucker factor can mount swiftly. If everything goes according to plan, you could arrive back at the field with as much as 4,000 pounds of fuel, but if anything comes up, that cushion could shrink to nothing in a hurry. The point is that with all the possibilities for consuming additional fuel, you certainly don't want to make any needless contributions.

Until engine runup, you and your RIO have been busy accomplishing individual tasks in preparation for flight, but starting then you become a team, informing one another of all factors that might influence the safety and success of the flight. The engines are brought individually to military power (full nonafterburning throttle) and checked for oil pressure, RPM, exhaust temperature, and fuel flow and then snap-decelerated to check fuel control rigging. The half-flap position used for takeoff opens the boundary-layer valves, ducting engine bleed air to the leading edge of the wing to add energy to the upper wing surface air. The increased lift allows the Phantom to slow to below 135 knots on landing approach, twenty knots slower than would be otherwise possible.

After you and your RIO have finished your own takeoff checks, you monitor your wingman's aircraft, noting his configuration and checking for leaks and missing or open panels. When he has done the same for you and signaled his readiness for flight, you draw the control stick full aft into your lap, whirl your fingers in a "wind-up" motion, and advance the throttles to 80 percent, checking instruments a final time. Bobbing your head forward, you release brakes and slide the throttles forward to the military stops, then outboard and midway forward in the afterburning range, leaving additional thrust for the wingman to maintain position.

No matter how many times you romp down the runway in burner—even at a high gross weight and

a reduced power setting—the sensation is terrific. Your feet try to lift from the rudder pedals under the tremendous acceleration, and the Phantom wants to squirt out from underneath you like a greased pig. With the stiff shock struts, you feel every crack and groove in the runway, and there is a slight shimmy as the stabilator begins to snatch air and the nose lightens. No sooner has the RIO confirmed 120 knots on the airspeed indicator than the nose gear is off the ground and you have to come forward on the stick to maintain a ten- to twelve-degree nose-high attitude. At 140 knots there is one last thud and you're airborne.

Bam. You slam the gear handle to the "up" stop with a vengeance, as if anything less would be insufficient to cause 3,000 psi of hydraulics to whisk away the gangly undercarriage in something less than two seconds. The nose picks slightly, and then it's time to send the flaps to their stowed position. You barely have time to scan the instruments before it's time to retard the throttles out of the afterburning range, leaving a couple percent of power as leeway for your wingman who is already sliding out to combat spread formation—a mile and a quarter abeam and stepped up a thousand feet.

During initial climb and cruise you have time to go through the weapons system checks to determine the status of the radar, AFCS (aircraft fire control system), and all the missiles. Your RIO runs through his BIT checks which show him what he can expect in the way of weapons system performance, while you check for confirmation lights on the missile status panel, switching from Sidewinder to Sidewinder, making sure each gives its characteristic tone. It is also a time for establishing a "howgozit" on fuel consumption and cruise performance. Aircraft can differ radically from one another, so it's a good idea to know how well yours conforms to the planned spec.

The tanker preceded you airborne by ten minutes, which gave him time to climb to 5,000 feet and establish his outbound course. As you level at

7,500 feet for the initial cruise, you've already sliced the distance to twenty-five miles and are running him down at the rate of three miles per minute. Seventy-five miles downrange you slide abeam the Herk, and almost simultaneously the A-4 flight checks in on frequency. It will be another twenty-five minutes and a total of 160 miles downrange before the A-4s rendezvous with the tanker and commence tanking. With two Scooters plugged in at a time, each scheduled to receive 2,500 pounds of fuel, the tanker will drag them another fifty miles, which gives them twenty miles of grace on the pushover point at Garnet.

Setting up a racetrack pattern around a slow-mover like the KC-130 requires a little finesse. You want to keep yourself between him and the anticipated threat area as much as possible while maintaining a position close enough to counter a pop-up attack. Moreover, you want to keep your speed up so you can maneuver while staying wings-level long enough to adequately search for intruders. These are contradictory requirements, so as with almost everything else in aviation, you have to compromise—380 knots instead of 420; three miles abeam to the east, one to the west; three miles upwind, five astern; and hard turns at either end. While you're still heavy, you're gulping down more than a quart of fuel with every heartbeat.

On the downwind leg of the fifth orbit, the Sky-

hawks slide by, 2,000 feet low and in the process of joining prior to stabilizing on the tanker. Since the original check-in, not a word has been spoken on the radio. In pairs, the Skyhawks plug in, tank up, and withdraw, and when the second section completes the procedure, the entire flight slides off to the right and departs on course. After the A-4s clear, the tanker shears away in a right-hand turn, taking up a heading to the emergency refueling point.

Checking your fuel gauge, you note that you've already burned 7,500 pounds of fuel, leaving you with 14,500 pounds to complete the remaining ninety minutes or so of flight—no problem. On the new heading, the flight settles out into a routine of six-minute cycles around the tanker. Fifteen minutes of drilling around has put you five minutes from the tanker orbit point, and after twenty minutes on station, it'll be time to head for the barn.

"Mad Dog One, I've got two targets bearing zero-three-five for sixty-five and sixty-eight nautical miles climbing through angels one-zero [10,000 feet] heading southeast at six-two-zero knots. Negative squawk." The dispassionate voice of the Wayside controller slices your complacency like a knife. It's almost certainly a raid on the tanker, and at the present rate of closure—over eight miles per minute with the angle-off—it will take the bogies eight minutes to run the tanker down. Even if the tanker were to abandon its mission and turn tail, the intercept time would be less than ten minutes, so it's important to engage the raid as far out as possible.

"Roger, Wayside. Mad Dog Two come port hard to a heading of zero-four-zero. Set one point two mach." With that, you drop the nose steeply down, carving the turn well below the horizon with the burners lit. The plan is to kick the bogies out to the left, setting up a beam Sparrow attack. That way, if you get a late ID (target identification) or a missile failure, you'll be able to continue on with a stern attack, forcing the intruders to respond to you and ignore the tanker.

"Out of turn, your bogies will be ten degrees left

for fifty-two miles, level at angels one-five heading two-one-five degrees." Even before you've rolled out on heading, you see the radar acquisition symbols move as if by magic to the left edge of the repeater screen and slide smoothly down to embrace a little square blip. The magic is in the hands of the RIO as he maneuvers his joystick until he finds the target and achieves lock-on. Suddenly the display changes, and you're looking at the attack presentation, comprised of the large range-rate circle with a V_c (closing velocity) gap in it; a smaller aircraft steering circle in the center, accessed by the aim dot, which is presently off to the left by half an inch; a horizon line running between the one o'clock and eight o'clock positions indicating a steep nose-down left turn; the "B-sweep" line moving in from the left, showing the antenna's horizontal train angle; and finally on the right margin, the "El-strobe," in the three o'clock position, showing that the bogies are level, by the straight-and-level antenna vertical train angle.

"Searchlight, I've got a contact seven left for fifty-four, closing at thirteen hundred knots."

"That's your bogey."

"Roger. I'll take a Judy." You've taken responsibility for the intercept.

"Mad Dog Two, have you got contact?"

"That's affirmative. Two's got two targets ten left for forty-seven and fifty."

"Dash One will VID [make a visual identification] and engage the leader. You take number two."

The Phantom goes through the sound barrier without a protest. About the only thing you notice is that the stick seems firmer. The mach needle slides smoothly up to the 1.2 mark and you have to come back on the power halfway to the burner detent. The acceleration cost over 1,500 pounds of fuel, leaving you with 11,200 pounds remaining, and you're still two minutes away from turning into the attack, guzzling better than two gallons every second.

"The leader's down to twenty-eight miles. Two's

dropped back a little—now four miles in trail." In the last minute the RIO has gone in and out of lock half a dozen times, searching for other aircraft that might be lurking in the weeds. You scan the area where the bogies should be using an off-the-shelf deer rifle spotting scope, but you can't find them.

Four Sparrows tuned and ready . . . lights and tones on all the Sidewinders . . . fuel 5,000 pounds . . . thirty left for fifteen miles . . . where is that turkey . . . stand by to bring him to the nose.

At twelve miles and still closing at more than fifteen miles a minute, it's time to commence the VID.

Nose level . . . seventy degrees bank . . . El-strobe shows five-degrees high . . . eight miles twenty left . . . should see him now.

The closure drops to under 900 knots as the B-sweep centers. Then you see him—an indefinite shape that grows perceptibly with each second. Now you're past the perpendicular, turning onto the bogey's course inside four miles.

Eyeballs do your thing . . . tighten the turn . . . speed's dropping . . . up the wick.

Then it's right there, bigger than life. MiG-23—Flogger E—with variable-geometry wings, two heat-seeking missiles, short-range radar, a gun, and a pair of Apex all-aspect semiactive radar-guided missiles. The radar attack presentation grows to its maximum diameter indicating the optimum range,

and begins its inexorable collapse until it reaches the minimum-range Break-X, but the aim dot is planted firmly in the center.

"Fox-one on the lead. You're cleared to fire, Two."

"Roger, Mad Dog. I'm taking a fox-one on number two."

At first there's nothing but the soft clunk of the missile-bay ejector foot kicking the chunky Sparrow clear of the aircraft.

Nothing's happening . . . it's going to be a dud . . . fire a second bird.

But before you can squeeze the trigger another time, off she roars in an awesome trail of smoke and sound. The Flogger's burner lights—a flash of fire and a ribbon of smoke confirm the launch of his missile—and he pulls around nose-high to counter the attack. Without thinking, you break hard to the right and punch off a volley of chaff. His missile tails off in a ballistic arc, while ahead, target and missile merge, and then . . . nothing. Instead of a ball of flame and debris, you're looking at the business end of an aircraft that is very capable of eating you up.

Max afterburner . . . relax the pull and go for separation.

There's a flurry of activity out at your two o'clock, but there's no time to think about it now. The Flogger passes by less than a quarter of a mile off your left side, now nearly inverted as he struggles to get his nose down to build back to maneuvering speed. Wings level with nose slightly low, throttles bent around the afterburning stops, you race away, straining to gain enough distance to turn back and nail your opponent with another shot. For the moment, nothing else exists.

"Dash Two's got a crispy critter."

Good. Your wingman's missile did its job. Unloaded, your speed has climbed to 1.4 mach, more than 300 knots faster than your opponent, who has bled his airspeed away in a vain attempt to get a shot. Ten more seconds to get enough separation,

then secure the burner and haul back over your left shoulder.

Select heat [Sidewinder mode] . . . keep it coming . . . right over the top . . . find the mother.

Approaching the zenith of its arc back to the south, the Phantom slows to subsonic, and without increasing backstick, you jump to over five g's. Nose-high through the inverted position, your eyes are dazzled by the midafternoon sun, but you resist the urge to slam your tinted visor down. You know where your opponent has to be, but picking him out against the ground can be hard.

"There he is, coming into our ten-thirty low." Your RIO is grunting as much from the strain of twisting around to look out the rear as from the gut-wrenching acceleration, but it's his help in acquiring the enemy that makes his two extra eyeballs worth a thousand times their weight in ECM gear.

The Flogger is trying gamely to get back around, but in his hurry to turn, he's run himself out of energy. Realizing his predicament, he's leveled his wings and lowered his nose in a last gasp attempt to disengage, but it's too late. No sooner have your brought your nose to his fuselage than the buzzing tone in your headset confirms the Sidewinder seeker head's lock-on. At three quarters of a mile with a 120-degree crossing angle, the—23 is easy prey.

"Fox-two." This time there's no doubt as the Flogger disintegrates at almost the instant the Sidewinder cornholes his exhaust cone. "Mad Dog lead turning to one-nine-five and climbing to angels two-nine. Say state, Dash Two."

From initial contact to conclusion, the engagement has taken less than seven minutes, but in that time you've gone through 9,800 pounds of fuel, leaving you with enough to get back to base with a scant 950 pounds, sufficient for one go-around, if the gauge is accurate, but only if you climb immediately to the optimum cruising altitude and descend at idle to the field. Some days you work to earn your flight pay.

Hercules (KC-130)

The venerable Hercules is flown by some sixty air forces around the world; the Marine KC-130 designation denotes combined tanker and cargo capability.

Do you remember the old question, What could possibly replace the DC-3? It remained unanswerable for the nearly two decades that Donald Douglas's miracle of aluminum, steel, rubber, and neoprene reigned supreme in the skies of the world. Sure, you could hang more engines and call it a C-54, or carve out a more cavernous belly to hold more and heavier cargo like the bunch of plug-uglies sporting numbers from C-82 to C-124. The Corps stumbled around the sky in the C-119 "Flying Boxcar" (two ADs [Douglas Skyraiders] flying wing on a Dempster Dumpster), but the hummer's rightful place in the affection of transport pilots the world over was never really challenged.

Then in 1955 on a blustery March day in Mar-

ietta, Georgia, Lockheed stood the medium-haul world on its ear with the delivery of the first C-130—an event from which it has yet to recover. Now the question is, What could possibly replace the Hercules? Until its successor leaps out of nowhere and shoulders old Herk into the history books, it will remain rhetorical. The prototype was ugly, looking as if it had barely survived a run-in with Rocky Marciano, but luckily, someone in high places decided that for the Hercules to fulfill its destiny it would need a face-lift. Just what led some obscure designer to envision the finished product as having the proboscis of a dolphin tacked on the front of an Oscar Mayer wiener we'll never know, but one must suspect that divine intervention was part of the action.

The acquisition of the KC-130 marked a monumental, if somewhat obscure, milestone in the development of Marine aviation. You'd have thought that the arrival of the Hercules would have been greeted with grand huzzahs by the stovepipers—after all, the only refueling capability the Corps had was the buddy refueling store carried by A-4s, which was barely sufficient to cover Scooter needs and wholly inadequate to slake the thirst of the fighters—but its immediate impact was due to its transport capabilities, which were light-years ahead of the C-119's. In one way it was a shame. Trash hauling ceased to be an adventure. No more emergency diverts into Jonesboro, Arkansas, or Globe, Arizona. Suddenly you were stuck with the fact that you could leave Cherry Point bound for El Toro with the firm expectation that you would make it on the first try. If the Herk was a boon to the zoomies, it was even more to the grunts. All at once, the skies over Pendleton and Lejeune were filled with parachutes bearing all manner of men

Above: Rarely used JATO (jet-assisted takeoff) bottles wow the crowd at the annual El Toro Air Show.

Right: Pilots practice night landings in the ultra-realistic KC-130 cockpit simulator.

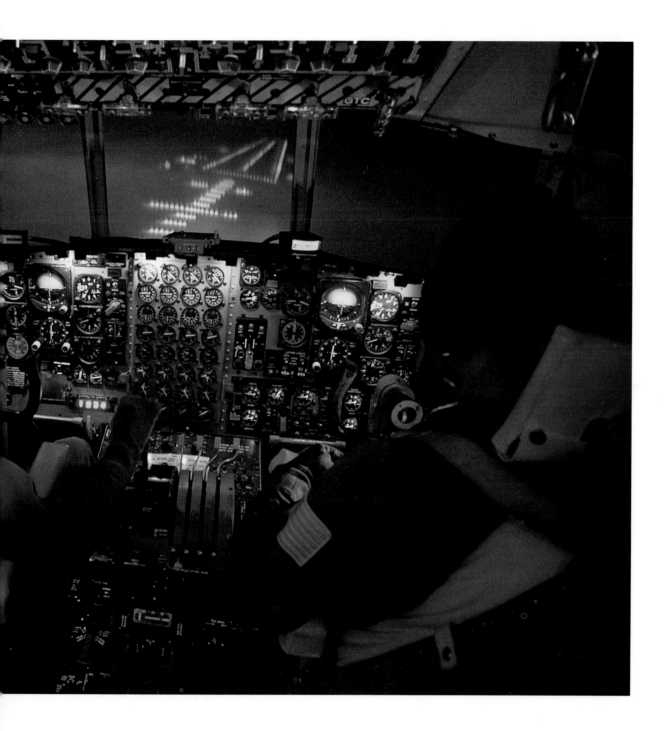

and equipment to the ground. Not only could the bird carry more weight and cube than anything the Corps had ever seen, it could do it more quickly and with greater reliability and safety than anyone had ever dared dream. Overnight, the Corps had moved into the big leagues as far as transports were concerned, and the grunts were not about to let the refueling mission rob them of this windfall.

Thus it was that during the early stages of Vietnam, Marine KC-130s flew around the countryside acting like their Air Force counterparts. Da Nang to Phu Bai to Quang Tri and back they went, then to the Philippines, Okinawa, and Japan. This was all well and good, but as the level of air operations increased—particularly those in the north and in Laos—the requirement for refueling increased. It may seem fundamental to people looking back on Vietnam with omniscience, but a great percentage of the Corps's missions could not have been attempted were it not for the presence of tanker support. Unheralded (except to those who accepted their succor on an almost daily basis) Marine Herks plied the skies between Chu Lai and Yankee Station for nearly a decade, transfusing all who were in need. If any resource was truly overworked in Vietnam,

Pudgy VMGR 352 Hercs squat on ramp at El Toro.

it was the Marine KC-130s. When they weren't playing gas station, they were transporting men, delivering material, and popping out flares wherever Marines were in action. Marine Herks got shot down by SAMs, blown out of the sky by triple-A, creamed on the runway by mortars, hosed down by ZPUs (23mm automatic cannon), and riddled with ground fire. No shrinking violets these guys; they were as tactical as any aircraft in the Corps, with more than their share of Purple Hearts to establish the point.

After a quarter century of service with the Corps, the KC-130 is more valuable than ever. One can hardly envision a tactical scenario in which success does not hinge on the plane's availability. The abilities to bypass the enemy's strength and exploit his weaknesses are powerful trump cards that are often underestimated, but they don't come about for free. Mobility and flexibility are the keys to success in expeditionary operations, and neither would be available without transport and tanker support. The kicker is distance. The multiplier factor varies from aircraft to aircraft and from mission to mission, but if you're talking about the tactical battlefield using fixed-wing fighter and attack aircraft, as well as helicopters of any category, the effects of range mount up quickly. Different studies have come up with different numbers—the requirement for anywhere from three to nine times the aircraft when the front is 250 nautical miles from the operating base—but regardless of the quantitative assessment, the penalties are real and, beyond some point, unacceptable. Helicopters can and do fly men and supplies from rear areas forward, but payload is payload so as fuel requirements mount, guns and grits are going to be the first to hit the cutting room floor. Sure FARPs (forward area refueling points) can be established along the route, but it takes sorties to keep them operating, so there's a limit to that as well. What it comes down to is that it takes fixed-wing transports with their superior range/payload capability to make a meaningful contribution in an extended resupply situation. And things are no different when it comes to maintaining tactical air cover for the troops. Every mile the operating base is from the FEBA imposes some penalty or another, and whether it is in response time, time on station, ordnance payload, or refueling support, it hurts. Of these, the last is by far the most tactically acceptable, but it too comes with a price tag.

The Hercules provides so many necessary services in a tactical situation—air refueling, troop and cargo insertion/resupply, tactical SAR, RGR (rapid ground refueling whereby it becomes a service station for other aircraft), casualty evacuation, and night flare delivery, to name a few—that demands on their limited numbers are enormous. It is little wonder they are primary targets in the enemy order of battle–knock out the Herks and you've chopped off Marine mobility at the knees. Because of their elevated status, they require fighter escort whenever they are within range of enemy aircraft.

We are used to thinking of troop and/or cargo delivery as a matter of picking up a load at airfield A and transporting it to airfield B at the other end of the line. That's pretty much how it worked in Vietnam and how you'd love to have it happen in the future. The trouble is, you don't know for sure that there are going to be airfields where you're going, and even if there are, they're liable to be the heavily defended areas you'd like to avoid. Air delivery by parachute is an alternative that has been successfully employed in the past, but it is also by nature a risky business. So many factors must be assessed that no commander can look at this method without some amount of fear, and when the unexpected is thrown in to boot, he'd probably do about anything to go another way.

Pioneered by helicopters and fueled by the mounting appreciation for the AV-8s STOVL capabilities, the use of austere and minimally improved sites—often no more than remote sections of roadway—is receiving increased attention. The

KC-130 awaits thirsty CH-53E helos in Southern California tanker track.

establishment and maintenance of such facilities is heavily dependent on KC-130 support. Given adequate width for its fifteen-foot landing gear track, lateral clearance for the 132.6-foot wingspan, enough length to recover and launch over obstacles along its arrival and departure flight paths, and adequate weight-bearing properties of the roadway, support of an austere base is within the aircraft's capabilities. As a rule of thumb, if a truck can drive over a surface without rutting it, a KC-130 can fly onto and off of it. Continued high-weight operations might begin to degrade the surface, but relocating or laying down matting could stabilize the situation.

Over the years, improved brakes, stronger wings and wheel struts, and increased power have led to increased short/unimproved runway performance. Considering that the aircraft will be landing heavy, off-loading, and taking off at a reduced weight, it is fairly safe to assume that a strip that will permit a safe arrival will be adequate for departure, but in situations in which such factors as high altitude and/or temperature degrade takeoff performance to such an extent that normal departure is impossible, engine output can be augmented by the use of JATO (jet assisted takeoff) rocket motors, each of which deliver 8,000 pounds of thrust for over ten seconds. If that isn't sufficient, it is hard to envision how anything else could operate out of the strip either, so it probably isn't a consideration. Let's take a look at a remote base and the role of the KC-130 in its establishment and operation.

In a typical operation, a reconnaissance unit would be put into the area to sniff things out. If the area was found to be secure, troops would be landed (by transport or by helicopter) to set up a perimeter in preparation for the establishment of a base. Assuming that an area existed (we're postulating that this is a roadway, but it could apply to other unimproved areas as well) whose location, width, clearway, length, and composition were sufficient for the task, transports would commence rotating in the men, material, facilities, and consumables. To give you some appreciation for the level of effort here, something on the order of three dozen KC-130 loads are required to embark a MACS unit;

One of the most unnerving feats in modern aviation: a Navy CH-53E helo refuels from a KC-130 of El Toro's VMGR 352. Rotor closes within fifty feet of the Herc's tail.

so when you understand that this is but one relatively small supporting unit from among many, you can begin to appreciate the complexity of the operation. We'll come back to the austere base later, but at the moment, your KC-130s are operating out of the main base in support of aviation activities.

It's dark as you head out onto the flight line. In its murky green-gray paint, the bird is a hazy silhouette against the dim horizon, and with the ramp down the tarmac behind is bathed in soft red from the interior lighting. Two crewmen with white flashlights inspect the tail section for leaks or damage, while a third stands on a ladder peering at the back of the air refueling pod. A maverick gust carries the sweet scent of warm turbine exhaust, the residual perfume of the plane's ground power unit, whose monotonous whistle wavers on the uncertain night wind. Mars is low to the east, while high overhead lies the luminous swathe of the Milky Way. "There is something about the desert . . ." you start to tell yourself, but you trip on a tie-down ring which nips your poetic excursion in the bud.

Night low-altitude refueling. Even the words seem contradictory, but it's becoming the rule rather than the exception. Because of the distances involved, fighter and attack aircraft maintain an around-the-clock vigil, orbiting thirty miles from the FEBA, on call in case they're needed. To maintain station, they have to be topped off every forty-five minutes. Relief for the fast-movers is effected every two hours, but not so for you. The tanker stays there for six hours, so that, counting the hour out and the hour back to and from the orbit point, the sun will be an hour old before you're on the deck again. It's routine and monotonous on one hand, but it's the kind of mission that can go to worms in a hurry if the action heats up.

There's a crew of six for these night gaggles— you and your copilot, a flight engineer, and a navigator on the flight deck, and two observers in the rear, one of whom is a radio operator while the other is a mechanic. On long flights, particularly overwater, the radio operator would remain on the flight deck, but because on this flight you will be handling all of the communications on UHF frequencies, he can be released to perform observer duties. The aircraft is configured with a high-speed drogue on the starboard side for the jets to plug into and a low-speed drogue on the port for the CH-53Es. The difference is in the size of the basket. The low-speed basket is considerably larger, not to make a bigger target, but to provide sufficient drag at the lower speed to keep the hose taut. At 120 knots (CH-53 refueling speed) the high-speed hose would be hanging limply in trail, while 180 knots is more than enough speed to tear the low-speed basket right off, hence the dual configuration.

The flight deck of the KC-30 is so spacious you could load it up with a whole squadron of A-4 pilots. Despite the fact that every year seems to bring forth its share of add-ons, the cockpit is remarkably uncluttered and the visibility is terrific. Over the nose, you can see the ground twenty feet ahead, and to the side you can look almost straight down because of the lower windows. With the prestart checklist completed, you make sure that the props are clear and that the fire extinguisher bottle is manned before directing start air from the ground power unit to the left inboard engine. One by one the four T-56 Allison turboprops come to life, shaking the airframe with the violence of their propwash. In the chocks, the Herk pounds the air with a rasping roar, but once the paddles start producing thrust for taxi, things become shockingly silent, bringing images of stalking death in the stealthy whirlings of four-bladed scythes.

Turning onto the taxiway, you are startled by a sudden flare, as a pair of Phantoms roar past in an ear-numbing madhouse of noise, their passage marked by parallel shafts of yellow gore that sear the runway before tearing free. It is Skidrow flight becoming airborne, preceding you to the orbit.

The cargo compartment contains a giant fuel tank lashed to the floor by vice-grip hold-downs. Canvas-covered troop seats line both sides of the compartment, stowed in their "up" position to leave clearway along the sides of the tank. During refueling, the observers will man the portholes in the aft doorways just forward of the ramp hinge, but for takeoff the radio operator is on the flightdeck while the mechanic monitors the cargo compartment. Outbound on the taxiway, you work your way methodically down the checklist so that by the time you round the corner at the approach end of the runway, you ask for and receive clearance to take position on the runway for runup checks without having to come to a stop.

The props are already turning at takeoff rpm, so by advancing the throttles you increase the engines' torque, causing the props to take a healthier bite of air. Once the engines are fully loaded, the propeller pitch controllers seek to maintain constant engine speed, responding to differences in airspeed and atmospheric changes with corrections

KC-130 turbine undergoes periodic inspection in VMGR 352 hangar.

to the bite. Following brake release, the airplane gathers momentum with surprising speed. It's not what you'd call a rush, rather the acceleration seems inexorable. You can feel it in your back against the seat, while in the rear, the observer finds himself sliding sideways along the nylon seat toward the ramp. Just at lift-off there seems to be a slight reluctance to part company with the ground, and then you're away and climbing smoothly into the dark. After the gear have thumped up and the flaps howled their way to the stops, you are stuck with the monotonous drum of the engines and the crisp sidetone of radio transmissions.

"Wayside, Volleyball One-One is outbound the zero-three-zero degree radial at two thousand five hundred feet estimating Hotel in five-zero minutes."

"Roger, Volleyball, radar contact. Remain this frequency. Break-break. Skidrow flight clear of traffic. Come port to zero-two-zero."

In low-altitude cruise you're burning in the neighborhood of 6,000 pounds of fuel per hour—a quarter of a mile per gallon at 225 knots—which is really fuel-efficient when you think about how much frontal area you're pushing through the sky. The fuel spec would be better at a higher altitude, but with the relatively short distance to the refueling track, it's not critical, so you'll stay low to remain masked from enemy radars. The enemy's not liable to go after the fighters, but you're a different matter. From here on out you plan to stay off the radio and maintain a low profile unless something out of the ordinary comes up.

The plane yaws slightly to the right as the starboard drogue catches the airstream and slides slowly aft, dragging its hose behind it. The pressure in the response system is good, and the status lights confirm that refueling can commence. Throughout the period you will dispense 4,500 pounds of fuel to each of eight aircraft for a total giveaway of 36,000 of the roughly 88,000 pounds of takeoff fuel. Between cruise and loiter segments, you should burn

another 42,000 pounds, leaving an additional 10,000 pounds to cover contingencies.

It isn't an easy job to sit there and wait for a flight of fighters to materialize out of the murk and then hope they get on and off the drogue without incident. It's not easy nor is it glamorous ("There I was at 2,500 feet, in pitch darkness sitting there fat, dumb, and happy while some hotshot in his fighter skewered my basket with his probe"), but without the KC-130s you can forget about fighting this kind of war. It's either that or find a place to fight it that has 10,000 feet of hard-surface runway close at hand.

"Formation lights coming up on the port side, sir." They're too far aft for you to see them, but the observer has them in sight as they slide in and stabilize at your seven o'clock position for a thousand feet.

"They're in observation position, sir. Are they cleared to continue?"

"Cleared to plug." The observer shines the Aldis lamp, showing one steady white light, and after a slight hesitation, the wingman crosses under the lead fighter and slides behind the tanker's tail. It reappears on the right side, lined up behind the drogue. The light on the tail of the refueling pod is amber, indicating to the receiver that the drogue is ready. To the observer, it is almost dreamlike. The shape of the plane is indistinct in the darkness, causing the phosphorescent formation lights—strips of soft green on the tail and on the forward fuselage below the cockpit—to leap out in bold relief. The apparition bobs up and down with a steady, hypnotic cadence, but what is really spooky is that the pilot's cockpit, bathed in red, seems to float free from anything around it, as if it came from a distant time and place and got locked into the wrong scene. The pilot's head swivels with random jerks. Close to the drogue, the cockpit/plasma bubble goes into a feeding frenzy, thrashing up and down and sideways until contact is made with the hose. The rhythmic bobbing returns and the scene makes sense again, but it leaves you a little uneasy.

"Contact, sir." He didn't need to tell you. It isn't just the force of the six-knot closure against the basket that you feel, but also the action of the response system in the refueling pod that reeled the hose quickly in to keep it from bending in the middle and snapping back. The refueling panel, programmed to dispense 4,500 pounds, shows fuel flow, so for the time being things are under control. You can relax a little and allow the autopilot to handle things.

For the Phantom pilot, who is concentrating on maintaining position on the dimly lit tanker, things can get pretty spooky as well. With everything outside of his own cockpit cloaked in darkness, his only attitude reference is the tanker's wing. Essentially, its sharp, straight line, the upward crank of the fuselage at the ramp hinge (noted in his peripheral vision only if it starts to change position), and the curving hose are the whole world as far as he is concerned. Because he has no real horizon, the tanker could roll into a bank and he would probably never know it except through the slight disturbance in his inner ears. It is not uncommon for receiver pilots to lose all track of up and down, achieving such a severe case of vertigo that they remain disoriented until they're back on the ground. In extreme cases, vertigo can produce nausea, and about the only option at that point is to head the plane for the base, set it on autopilot, and pray that you don't get sick.

The green light on the pod turns to white, indicating that fuel flow has ceased, and the Phantom backs out. At release he's a little lower and to the right of the trail position of the drogue, imparting a violent whip that goes through several cycles before damping itself out. The autopilot fights the oscillation with minute corrections, as if to scold the fighter as he backs away into the void. Soon you feel the leader make contact, and after scanning the refueling panel for malfunctions, you settle back once more.

The night grinds by. Wayside calls one flight to contact a FAC for a mission. Another flight orbits, refuels, orbits, and is relieved on station without incident. There are terse communications on the radio, but these do little to check the growing anticipation of tanking the last flight and heading for the barn. You unstrap and pace the flight deck for a while. In days gone by, you'd have smoked a pack of cigarettes by now, but since you quit there's not even that solace. The coffee is tepid and the water tastes like straight fluoride even though you know they cut it one-to-one with water. You scan the flight engineer's panel for anything unusual, but there's not the slightest anomaly to occupy so much as a moment's notice, and there's nothing going on at the navigator's station to draw your attention. Finally, as the eastern horizon begins to grow yellow, the last aircraft has had its way with you and backed out, and before the hose has retracted halfway into the pod, you've reefed the bird into a forty-five-degree bank to the southwest and headed for home.

"We'll make it back ten minutes early," you note with pleasure, but in the same breath you ask, "What's on the schedule for today?"

Chapter 5
Forward Operating Base

With a major battle shaping up 250 miles from the main operating base, it has become necessary to establish an austere forward base on a section of highway forty miles behind the FEBA. Imagine the surroundings. The section of road is in a low area between rolling hills. Ten miles northeast is a hill rising 5,500 feet, giving it a commanding view of the countryside in all directions out to a distance of fifty miles. Until now it wasn't a transportation and communication center, not a twenty-four-hour-a-day hotbed of activity, not even a wide spot in the road. It was a lonely stretch of concrete out in the middle of nowhere, accustomed to seeing two to three vehicles a day maximum. But now look at it. Equipment of all sorts races around dirt roads cut through the sparse woodland by bulldozers, which are busy night and day making room for the thousands of tons of material and equipment that pour in from an endless line of transports. It's a colossal undertaking that boggles the mind. *Why* anyone would build a base out here is more than enough to bewilder those tasked with doing it. Contemplating the *how* and *with what* is the kind of thing that makes planning staffs shudder.

In concert with mile-long truck convoys snaking their way up from the beachhead, Air Force C-141s and C-5s along with Marine KC-130s, CH-46s, and CH-53s leap-frog men, equipment, and supplies into position and, even before much of the tenting has arrived, troop support mission commences. The strip is home for eight-plane detachments of AH-1Js, AH-1T(TOW)s, UH-1Ns, OV-10A/Ds, and AV-8C/Bs. Elements of the two CH-46 Sea Knight and CH-53 Super Stallion squadrons operate from the field, and rounding things out are a MASS, a forward element of a MACS, a MATC (Marine air traffic control) detachment, one battery of a LAAMBN (light antiaircraft missile battalion), and a FAAD (forward antiaircraft defense) unit. Just a list of the line items required to get the base operational is staggering, until you begin to see that you're not talking about ones and twos of each, but perhaps hundreds or thousands and more. Then it becomes incomprehensible.

Like the circus, you've got tents and pegs and dunnage. There's food and furnishings and stoves, mess trays, utensils, and coffee mugs. There are prime movers and trailers and support vehicles whose names, much less functions, are unknown to all but those who use them. You could go on and on, milking the circus analogy to the limit, and then you'd begin the litany in earnest. No lions and tigers or clowns (you hope). Instead it's bombs and bullets and spare parts for the 25mm cannon, pallets of ordnance tools and equipment, and boxes of tires and brake parts. There are two dozen radar and fire control vans that will house operators and controllers and equipment for the MACS, MASS, MATC, and LAAMBN units that are busily setting up shop.

While matting is laid and camouflage netting stretched to create "hides" for the aircraft, tinkertoy scaffolding for a forty-foot-high control tower

Marines operate devastating Hawk (*above*) and shoulder-fired Stinger (*right*) missiles for antiair defense.

is put together and levered into the vertical. Berms are bulldozed to contain rubber bladder fuel tanks, into which the first batch of the precious fuel is being transferred from a KC-130. Fields of fire are cleared, and key locations surveyed and ranged for mortar and artillery batteries. Water wells are drilled, and radar antennae assembled and emplaced on high ground. Low-power lighting and landing aids and runway length markers are installed and tested, and navigation beacons and approach radar gear are fired up and aligned. Helicopters cycle in and out, while high above, fighters roam the sky in search of enemy aircraft. Tools and spares and forms and manuals and cradles and dollies and jack stands and drill presses appear like mushrooms following a heavy rainstorm. A field surgery unit comes off a transport's tailramp in the grasp of a forklift, followed by an avionics repair van and power supply. Latrines are dug, a garbage dump cleared. Rows of concertina festooned with combat ration tins surround the perimeter, creating a visible and painful spoor to any who would violate the territory.

Atop the hill, antennae, erected from pieces, scan the heavens, looking for trouble. Some bob up and down, and others whirl around a spot. Some look fixedly at a particular point, and some are doing nothing for the moment. But all have their purpose. The big flat panel rotating on a massive shaft belongs to the MACS who uses it to control friendly aircraft in the area. Reaching out 250 miles, it watches for enemy aircraft that might try to penetrate and strike the ground troops at the front, the friendly aircraft supporting the operation, or even the forward base and its facilities. The control vans with their computers, consoles, and controllers sit on a ledge a thousand feet downhill, even farther down is a similar cluster housing the MASS equipment.

Even before the base is ready to conduct combat operations, the MASS unit has the DASC (direct air support center) going full tilt, its radar controlling air strikes in the TAOR. It seems fantastic, but a controller, seated comfortably in front of a console, has the ability to guide a distant aircraft to its target at night or foul weather, maneuvering it into position to release its ordnance. This is the way to wage war—miles from the antiaircraft defenses with a cup of coffee to keep the hands warm. The DASC complements the MACS, directing offensive air operations, and as with the MACS and MATC squadrons, many of the controllers are WMs (women Marines), introducing interesting speculations as to the role of women in combat.

Just below the top of the hill, the LAAMBN battery has set up its spaces with cables leading up to the missile launch sites, each with three Hawk missiles locked to the rails. The Hawk is quite a system, able to seek out and destroy a target that has been acquired either by radar or through its optical system. Menacing looking in its desert paint scheme, the hummer is able to go zero to mach-3 in little more than its own length and still out turn the most maneuverable aircraft in the sky. If you know a Hawk is on its way, the time to eject is *now,* because regardless of which way you're heading, *never* is coming down the pike at a half mile per second.

The insides of the various control vans are kept cool and in perpetual twilight. The spatter of terse communications against the muted background frequency hum of the electronic equipment is in sharp contrast with the roar of the power supply and air conditioning gear on the other side of the door. The MACS complex is made up of five interconnected vans with display consoles and a status board. Controllers sit before screens containing both raw radar plots and computer-generated symbols that help them keep track of the area. At will they can call up different screens that range from a full 360-degree plan view of the 250 mile area down to small, pie-shaped sectors with blown-up images. Cultural, natural, and tactical features can be displayed, and by touching the screen the controller can get an immediate readout of such things as an aircraft's altitude, airspeed, and heading, as well

as the time, heading, and distance to intercept another aircraft or position over the ground.

The SAD (senior air director) monitors all the positions, and if an "unknown" appears, he will assign it to a controller. All friendly aircraft carry a radar transponder (IFF standing for "identification, friend or foe"), which transmits a coded pulse each time it is interrogated by a friendly radar. If the preassigned code is correct, the controller knows the aircraft is friendly, but if it is incorrect or if the aircraft is not responding (known as "squawking"), then the bogey is treated as a potential "hostile" that must be identified before it can be fired at. On the rare occasion when the controller knows a blip is a "bandit," he can pass the raid to the fighters or missile battery and, with concurrence of the SAD, clear them to fire without an ID.

The LAAMBN battery is set up a little differently. The TCO (tactical control officer) and his assistant monitor a large console displaying the MEZ (missile engagement zone). When a raid is passed to LAAMBN by the TACC (or if a pop-up raid

enters the MEZ in a manner that satisfies the "rules of engagement" criteria for missile launch), the TCO goes from "missiles tight" to "missiles free" and assigns it to one of two firing control operators. The designated operator accepts and locks up the target, confirming the acquisition with a readout of pertinent information such as range, airspeed, and whether the raid is within the missile's envelope. It is the TCO who determines how many missiles to expend and at what point. His command might be, "Alpha [the designated] section, shoot . . . look . . . shoot," and he confirms his order by switching from "cease fire" to "resume fire," on his console, which causes a flasher button in front of the appropriate fire control operator to pulse. After firing the first missile, the operator can watch on both a TV monitor and the radar as the missile tracks

downrange. If the radar breaks lock, he can still guide the Hawk to the target with the optical tracker, literally driving it on a collision course with the aircraft. This Hawk is a mean somebody.

First to arrive at the forward operating base are the transport helicopters, followed closely by the Cobras, Hueys, and Broncos. After an eighty-five-foot square pad has been cleared, matted, and accessed by taxiways, the Harriers arrived and set up shop in their camouflaged "hides." It is a momentous undertaking, but there's no waiting for someone to cut a ribbon or bless it with holy water; as soon as the birds are there, Camp Waller is operational.

CH-53D Stallions effortlessly sling-load 105mm howitzers over Camp Pendleton.

Harrier (AV-8)

With a deafening roar, it vaults out of its hiding place in the midst of a tree-stand, sucking its tandem gear up and tucking back the outriggers. Then it twirls as if on a turntable and stampedes away. You knew what it was going to do—you've watched it do its thing dozens of times—yet every time a Harrier acts like a bumblebee it blows your mind. Intellectually you're prepared, but intuitively you know that it's absurd. In hover it looks like a horizontal hummingbird just returned from Disneyland. Inlets protrude like comicbook earmuffs. Bulges and slots and antennae break the natural symmetry of aerodynamic design, confirming the subservience of form to function. Racks and conformal pods attach to the underside like space-age remora. It's sinister, as if the designers had made a pact with the devil. It's raw power held in critical balance by delicate control. It is, in fact, the single most interesting flying machine in America's military arsenal, and although it and its progenitors have been around for quite some time, the Harrier has barely begun to strut its stuff.

Lt. Col. Russ Stromberg drops in at Yuma after a night bombing hop during the OPEVAL (operational evaluation) of the new AV-8B Harrier.

Although the United States had its own VSTOL (vertical/short takeoff and land) programs, notably the Ryan X-13 and Bell X-14, the Harrier owes its existence to the British Hawker Siddeley P.1127 Kestrel. The P.1127 project began in 1957, and by 1965 the United States and Germany had joined the effort. Six Kestrels were sent to the United States for evaluation, but the program died for lack of interest. For its part, the RAF called for a redesign of the P.1127, and in mid 1966 the first Harrier flew, powered by a 19,000-pound static thrust Rolls Royce Pegasus engine. Over the next several years, powerplant development led to substantial improvements in aircraft performance.

The Marine Corps became interested in the Harrier in 1968, and received approval for the immediate purchase of 12 Group MK.3 Harriers in early 1969 with the balance of 110 to be delivered over the next several years. Though there were certain modifications needed to "Americanize" the birds, the entire fleet, redesignated the AV-8A, was built in England. The last delivery was in 1976. The first squadron to transition to the Harrier was VMA-513 in April 1971, followed by VMA-542 and VMA-231 in successive years. VMAT-203, the Harrier training squadron, received its aircraft in 1975. The first preproduction AV-8B built under license by McDonnell Douglas began flight tests in November 1981, in accordance with a contract that calls for a total of 331 aircraft by 1991. Prior to the first deliveries of the B-model, the remaining AV-8As were reoutfitted as AV-8Cs, the primary differences being in avionics, LIDs (lift improvement devices consisting of ventral strakes and a forward under-belly flap designed to contain the vectored thrust exhaust), ECM gear (passive antennae plus flare and chaff dispensers), and provision for mounting of TERs (triple ejector racks) on the outboard pylons.

You can tell this is a no-frills aircraft. Everything (and there are a lot of add-ons) contributes to the VSTOL activity—swiveling exhaust nozzles, blow-in doors, bleed air horizontal and lateral flight controls, LIDs on the bottom of the fuselage, and gigantic engine inlets, to name a few. Just the way it hunkers tells you something strange is going on.

Far left: Harrier II at vertical touchdown. Lift-improvement devices (LIDs) beside main landing gear focus engine thrust and keep hot exhaust from re-entering jet intakes.

Left: Small handle to right of pilot's hand controls position of thrust vector nozzles (*right*).

Far right: AV-8B packs full bomb load in demo flight near McDonnell Douglas's St. Louis assembly plant.

The fuselage sits on a pair of centerline landing gear—a single swiveling nosewheel and tandem aft carriage—balanced by outriggers outboard on each wing, giving the Harrier outstanding rough terrain ground-handling capability.

Despite the complexity of the vectoring and re-action control systems, the Harrier is a fairly straight forward aircraft from a maintenance point of view. Nonetheless, watching an engine swap can give you a jolt. After the aircraft has been put in a cradle, wing and upper fuselage turtleback are removed as a section so the powerplant can be winched out the top. It's like a plastic model. If you want to have air refueling capability, you bolt a probe onto the top of the port intake. Want guns? Attach a pair of conformal pods to the belly. It's that kind of an airplane–if you don't need something for the mission, you take it off.

The Harrier can be configured with any of the conventional ordnance in the Marine Corps inventory. In addition to the provision for conformal gunpods, there are five hardpoints (seven on the AV-8B) from which stores can be hung. Varying with temperature and elevation, the AV-8A can launch with full internal fuel (5,060 pounds) 7,700 pounds of external stores in the STO (short takeoff) mode. By contrast, the AV-8B, with 7,500 pounds of internal fuel, can get airborne with 9,500 pounds of external goodies. Though vertical takeoff is possible in either aircraft, the activity can impose range and or payload penalties. The more accurate acronym is STOVL (short takeoff/vertical land), which is actually the way Marines envision operating the aircraft. In the AV-8B with full internal fuel, you can launch with twelve 500-pound bombs, cruise out 150 nautical miles, loiter for an hour, deliver the weapons, return, and land—a respectable mission profile.

The Harrier's true advantage lies in its ability to stay close to where the action is because it can operate from roadways, pads, grass fields, or whatever is at hand. Rapid ground turn-around coupled with short stage lengths to and from the target provide the battlefield commander with unprecedented coverage, a point driven home on May 19, 1980, when a six aircraft detachment of Harriers operating from an austere strip at MCALF (Marine Corps auxiliary landing field) Bogue, North Carolina flew 42 sorties in two hours and nine minutes, while delivering over 40,000 pounds of ordnance. In an evolution dubbed "surge ops" because of the ferocious burst of activity, VMA-542 was able to complete the exercise with no malfunctions or aborts, and the average time to service and rearm between flights was 6.4 minutes per aircraft. What makes this rapid turn-around possible is a proce-

Spectacular computerized flight simulator takes Harrier II pilot through the approach to a Marine LHA (landing/helicopter assault) mini-carrier.

dure known as "daisy-chaining," where one aircraft is recovered vertically on a separate pad, another is taxied clear of the landing pad, shut down, refueled and rearmed, while still another is launching back into the fray using the STO mode.

Cockpitwise, the Harrier is pretty conventional until you come to the VSTOL gear. The first thing that tells you something's up is the extra control handle on the throttle quadrant next to your left leg, with sector angle detents along the edge. This, the duct pressure gauge, and the nozzle position indicator are the basic tools for VSTOL operations. Before you go out and fly your first combat mission, it's probably a good idea to become familiar with how it works, starting with a little (very little) theory.

A conventional aircraft flies because as the engine propels the vehicle forward, airflow over the wing causes a pressure differential between the up-

Gung-ho XO of VMA 513 lets his license plate tell of his unique status.

C-Model Harrier packs 500-pound bombs over the Camp Pendleton range. The "C" is SLEP (Service Life Extension Program) version of the original British-built AV-8A.

Lt. Charlie Cantan (*center*), Royal Navy Falklands vet, explains British Harrier tactics used in South Atlantic air combat.

Original AV-8As and Cs require huge dollops of maintenance as they age. The improved B model will steadily replace the early Harriers in the next few years.

per and lower surfaces. This differential (whose value is a function of airspeed, wing shape, surface area, and angle to the relative wind) is called "lift," and if this happens to equal the aircraft's weight, it will sustain level flight. An increase in lift will allow you to climb, and conversely, a decrease in lift below your aircraft's weight will cause you to descend. This is the normal flight regime, the one in which the Harrier spends 95 percent of its time. It's the other 5 percent of the time that gets a little trickier, because you are substituting engine thrust for velocity-generated lift. The basic weight of the AV-8B is 12,750 pounds. The Rolls Royce Pegasus puts out 21,500 pounds of thrust, so if you top off the internal fuel tanks with all 7,500 pounds, bringing your gross weight to 20,250 pounds (giving you a 1.05 to 1 thrust-to-weight ratio), it should leap into the air, right? Well not quite because there are some losses in efficiency inherent in thrust vectoring and because, close to the ground, the engine breathes some of its heated exhaust, lowering thrust output still more. Vertical takeoff becomes possible on a standard day (72 degrees Fahrenheit and 29.92 inches barometric pressure) at 19,650 pounds gross weight. With the nozzles vectored to the fully vertical position and with zero wind velocity over the wing, the engine thrust alone opposes weight, and because the thrust is greater, the aircraft ascends. If you wish to hover, you reduce thrust until you stop going up. Reduce still more and you go back down. It is all there in your left hand.

The transition from ascent to normal flight is accomplished by rescheduling the thrust vectoring handle forward, allowing the aircraft to accelerate until it gains sufficient speed for the wing to produce lift. Thereafter you can rotate the nozzles to their full aft position and maintain altitude and airspeed by modulating the throttle and nose position. During transition from high speed to vertical flight, the operation is reversed except that because you are going from a flight regime with a broad envelope to an area of very prescribed limits, there are more caveats and checkpoints to consider. As the airspeed falls off, the aerodynamic controls become less and less effective, until they are finally supplanted by reaction controls, located on the nose and tail and on each wingtip. Activated by stick and rudder, engine bleed air is routed to the appropriate duct, where it is exhausted into the airstream. The most critical moment comes deep into the transition when, with both aerodynamic and reaction controls at work, an asymmetric yaw-roll coupling beyond control limits could develop. The culprit is a thing called intake momentum drag (an anti-weathercocking phenomenon acting to increase the yaw-roll disparity) which occurs when the aircraft is crabbed out of its relative wind. The answer is to align the aircraft into the wind—a condition confirmed by the fore and aft fairing of a vane in front of the windscreen—but if you begin to yaw, the solution is to pour the coals to the engine, unvector to accelerate, and make a go-around.

Despite the obvious advantages STOVL operations offer, the Harrier has been the center of controversy throughout the decade it has been in service. Proponents cite the innate flexibility in being able to base it nearly anywhere—on highway sections, hastily constructed aluminum matting pads, aboard assault ships—and because it is not tied to conventional runways, which are certain to be targeted, it is less vulnerable while on the ground. Additionally, vectored thrust gives the Harrier a certain amount of advantage in close-in maneuvering against conventional aircraft because it can be used to increase the Harrier's turn rate. One of the most effective uses of thrust vectoring comes at the top and bottom portions of a vertical fight. In a maneuver known as "flopping", the pilot vectors to get the nose pointed in the other direction, leaving the opponent trying to match the turn with aerodynamic controls and gravity.

Opponents point out the penalties STOVL operations place on payload, range, speed, and radar reflectivity. Aircraft, it is argued, operating from conventional bases can make up for this deficiency by carrying more ordnance farther, faster, and with greater loiter potential, and can do so while retaining greater overall mission flexibility.

There is truth in each of the allegations concerning the AV-8A, but the AV-8B with redesigned aerodynamics, increased payload and fuel capacity, and upgraded avionics and stability augmentation systems will make tremendous improvements in its mission capability.

Strip alert is not always the most pleasant of ways to pass the time, particularly if the weather is lousy. Hot, cold, or dusty, sitting in the cockpit waiting for something to happen can be a drag, but when it's raining and you've got nothing better to do than to watch droplets bead and roll down the canopy and windscreen, you begin to appreciate the full ramifications of the word "boredom." Bip . . . bip . . . bip . . . another river makes its way down the side rail. Occasionally, a drop splats on your kneeboard, turning your frequency and controller information into a soggy smudge. Just another half hour, you remind yourself, looking past the control stick shaft at the clock hiding at the base of the center console. For the twentieth time, you check that your number two battery is switched on, and then run up the radio sensitivity to make sure that the set is still on the line and, absorbing the blast of static, you return to your reflections on boredom. Actually, the weather isn't all that miserable—you are. Over in the tactical area forty miles to the northeast, the cloud coverage is three tenths based 6,000 feet above the ground. What you're seeing is the leading edge of a weak storm, and by nightfall it will be clear here and rotten in the TAOR.

Here is a rapidly constructed camp beside the small stretch of roadway that, in the two weeks since its development began, has grown to house an eight-plane detachment of Harriers, along with four OV-10 Broncos, twelve AH-1Js and Ts, eight UH-1Ns, two squadrons of CH-46s, and one squadron of CH-53Es.

All day, KC-130s with ramps agape have broken out of the goo, touched down to deposit pallets of cargo, and without stopping headed back for more supplies. From the first, the choppers have been going almost constantly, bringing in fuel and ordnance for the Harriers, toting artillery and equipment out to the troops in the field, and moving combat units from place to place. Still, aside from the transport activities at the base, little seems to be going on. Since an insertion of three companies earlier in the day, accompanied by two flights of Harriers that orbited the area in case of opposition, things have been quiet for the fixed-wing contingent. Only the Broncos have gone anywhere, cycling out and back, relieving one another on station. The operation appears to have been a dry run,

so you think about how tonight's B-rations are going to taste, but as visions of Gaines-burgers and red death well up before your eyes, the radio comes alive with a request for aircover from a troop commander to the DASC.

Batteries on . . . fire up the APU [auxiliary power unit to run the standby generator and spool the main engine] *. . . come on, turkey, get up to speed.*

As the APU comes up to speed, you flip the start switch to rouse the sleeping monster in the bowels of your aluminum and plastic toy. At once you feel a flow of light unsynched vibrations in your seat as the three-stage turbo fan stirs into life. The sudden activity catches your wingman's attention, and even before you can signal him to fire up, his engine, too, is turning.

"Two up" informs you that your wingman is standing by on TACC frequency.

"Birdman flight standing by for mission brief."

"Roger, Birdman, mission number Charlie Golf zero-six-one-nine. Proceed via Bravo, and Delta, to Contact Point Oscar with Cooler Two-Two on Orange. Contact Wayside on Green when airborne." Communications between friendly entities are crisp and clear, but to an eavesdropper, they would be unintelligible, being scrambled for transmission and reconstructed at the receiving end by the KY-28 secure voice equipment.

Even at idle, the engine's sound, buffered by bulkhead, Plexiglas, and acoustic helmet/headset, pounds on you like the roar of a waterfall. Displays light up and erect as you flip switches and scan instruments in preparation for the short taxi to the highway.

"Two's ready."

"Roger. Button Two." You barely nudge the throttle and you're in motion, the main gear and outriggers slapping across the cobbled aluminum matting. Tower, already alerted to the scramble, waves off an inbound transport, and you roll onto the roadway without stopping. Loaded with twelve 500-pounders, two gunpods, and two Sidewinders

apiece, you and your wingman take interval for individual takeoffs, using vectored thrust to limit
ground run to 600 feet. Prior to takeoff you have
to clear the FCU (fuel control unit) on the engine
by cycling three times between 27 percent and 55
percent, checking for an acceleration time on the
DDI (digital display indicator) of between 3.6 and
4.6 seconds. Retarding the engine to 50 percent,
you turn on the water switch (water increases thrust
not only by adding to the total mass flow through
the engine, but by cooling critical components allowing a higher jet pipe temperature) and watch the
rpms climb to 55 percent, after which you vector
the nozzles to ten degrees, set the STO stop at sixty
degrees, check the inlet guide vane and duct pressure gauges for proper readings, take a deep breath,
and ram the throttle to the detent. Just as the tires
start to skid, you release the brakes and you're away.
Zing.

The feeling is unlike that of any other airplane
in the Western world. It's not the thumping kick
in the tail you experience in afterburning airplanes.
It's rather like being in the grip of a powerful sling-
shot. It literally sizzles down the road, and before
it seems possible, you're ready to translate. If you
haven't already got your left paw on the nozzle lever, you're going to miss the whole thing. The instant you see ninety knots, you bang the nozzle
lever to the STO stop, and you're airborne—just
like that. No fuss. No messing around wondering,
"Do we really want to do this today?" None of the
waffling incidental to a normal swept-wing takeoff. Poof . . . it's magic, and if you don't start
nozzling out again, the bird will hang you out to
dry.

*Hold twelve units angle of attack . . . easy on
the rudders . . . rotate the nozzles full aft.*

In little longer than it takes to tell, the Harrier
has vaulted from the roadway, accelerated through
300 knots, drilled a hole through the deck of low
stratus, and stormed into the clear blue above.

"Birdman Two's airborne."

"Roger. Switch to Green."

Laser designator for computerized angle-rate bombing
system is visible in the nose of the AV-8B.

Harrier II plane captain sends his bird on its way at Cherry
Point.

104

The two-place TAV-8A must carry a "stinger" tail weight to counterbalance its heavier nose.

AV-8B pilot responds to plane captain's hand signals prior to taxi.

Leveled out at 2,500 feet and cruising along at 420 knots, your AV-8B is like any other garden variety Piper Cub, except that it's got great visibility and a bunch of neat displays to fiddle with. The steering indicator on the HUD is giving range and bearing information to Contact Point Bravo, using data from the INS (inertial navigation system) that, in the five minutes it will take to get to the target, should be accurate to fifty meters. The plan is to cross Bravo below 1,500 feet and continue down to hit Delta at 200 feet, so at ten miles you push the nose over and prepare for the attack phase.

"Birdman approaching Bravo, switching to button Orange."

"Two, roger."

On the DDI, you call up the weapons select and designate the stations to be used, the number of bombs to be dropped, their interval, and their fusing. Putting your head in the cockpit while you're on a collision course with the ground takes a little getting used to, but with the new displays it's a lot easier than it used to be. By the time the switches are set, you're passing 500 feet and the speed is now up to 480 knots.

"Cooler, this is Birdman at Bravo for your control." Cooler is an OV-10 FAC(A) (airborne FAC) assigned to cover Charlie Company (2d Battalion, 25th Marines).

"Roger, Birdman, we've spotted a mortar battery three-five-zero degrees for seven miles from Delta. If you make your final run-in on a heading of three-three-zero, it'll be on the forward slope of a small hill. Depart Delta on a heading of zero-three-zero for two miles and then turn to three-five-zero. This will keep you clear of enemy positions. On pullout from the target, the friendlies will be at your nine o'clock for two clicks [kilometers]. I'll mark with a Willie Pete [white phosphorus warhead] rocket."

"Roger, Cooler. I'll make a three-sixty [full circle] to set up and we can be on target at sixteen-fifteen."

"Cleared to continue, Birdman. Call Delta."

It's a perfect target for the ordnance and your equipment, but setting up for the attack is a bear as you bend back around close to the weeds. You've already set up the ordnance switches, but it's a good idea to check them over again.

Stations selected . . . fuse for nose-only retarded . . . one hundred forty millisecond release interval between bombs.

It will be an auto-TV release in which you acquire and designate the target with the TV symbol on the HUD. Your job is to maneuver the aircraft to place the target within the confines of a small computer-generated window that has been projected onto the combining glass (along with information relating to aircraft speed, altitude, angle of attack, and heading) and capture it with the TDC (target designation control) on the throttle. This will put you into the ball park, but through the wonders of optics you can be even more precise. Going to the TV magnification mode (resulting in a six-fold increase in resolution), you transfer your scan to the DDI and "sweeten" your aimpoint on the target using the TV slew control on the throttle. Returning to the HUD, you follow the steering commands, holding the bomb-release "pickle" depressed until the computer determines that the time is ripe to kick the bombs off in the sequence and interval that you selected.

The maneuver itself is a *pop-up offset roll,* ending with a ten-degree dive, releasing the twelve 500-pounders in their "retarded" mode at 600 feet. This means that as the bombs come off the rack, fins pop open at the back that act like parachutes, slowing them to allow the aircraft to draw well ahead and out of the bomb fragmentation pattern. Because the safety wires for the nose fuses are attached to the tips of the "Snakeye" fins, should the fins fail to deploy, the safing wires would not be withdrawn, and the bombs would fall as duds. If you wished to drop the bombs and have them detonate as "slicks," you would arm them in the "tail-only" mode. This way the nose-arming wires would remain with the bomb to hold the fins in their faired position and the bombs would be detonated by the tail fuses.

After the outbound leg from Delta, the turn to 350 degrees will provide you with just about the right offset so that after thirty seconds, when you pull up thirty degrees nose-high and roll inverted at 700 feet, the target should come into view above the starboard canopy bow at a mile and a half. There's a lot of science in prosecuting an attack, but if that were all, you'd be better off staying at home and letting the widgets do the job. The maneuver, which started out as an exercise in kinesthesia and application of practiced control deflections, becomes increasingly a work of art as the attack progresses. The crossover comes when you're poised in mid leap, fighting to maintain your orientation in the rush of things, while searching for traces of the mortar positions against an unfamiliar backdrop.

Hillside . . . arroyo . . . smoke . . . where's the target from the smoke?

You haven't picked it up for sure, but you can't wait until you do. In almost any other endeavor, you could call for a timeout and review the situation. Not here where there is only the *now*—the past and future belonging to the world of those about to become very dead. Adding backstick, you pull the nose back below the horizon, becoming more frantic in your search. Then you see them—a series of earthwork scars running away from you, aligned almost perfectly with your final line of flight—and as if by magic you've parked the acquisition symbol dead center on the line and blipped the TDC. It isn't magic, and neither is the odd sensation that you've done this all before. In training you've rehearsed for this moment a thousand times—a different target perhaps, but the pattern is the same. The moment that Cooler gave you the target description, you began etching an image of a mortar battery into your vision of the run. From there on it was a matter of matching up the real world with your preconception. The rest of the run could already be history, except that it's the pay-off.

Roll . . . keep it centered . . . drive the pickle right out the bottom of the stick grip . . . there they go!

"Birdman's off, coming port to two-four-zero."

"Dash Two's in hot."

It has been ten minutes since launch when the last of your wingman's bombs detonates—fifteen since receiving the scramble—and counting the time it will take to return and land, refuel, and rearm, the whole excursion will have taken less than an hour. Most of this can be attributed to proximity, but there are other factors as well. The INS provides such accurate location information that you don't have to waste time groping around, even when you're down in the weeds. Another new feature in the AV-8B is the AWLS (all-weather landing system), which takes data supplied by a ground-based transmitter and displays heading and glideslope information right on the HUD. Together, the INS and AWLS allow the Harrier to be flown quickly to the landing area at night or in bad weather, arriving at a point to transition to vertical flight. Finally, because the bird will be flown to a spot, there is no time lost commencing refueling and turn-around activities.

Detaching your wingman to take his landing interval, you hit a five-mile "initial" at 1,500 feet altitude with gear and flaps set and engine water switch on. The first part of the approach is the same as for any aircraft, establishing a courseline and glideslope inbound to the landing spot. After breaking out of the clouds, you continue until you arrive at the "key"—a half mile from the landing pad where you commence transition. Selecting forty degree nozzle deflection, you slow to 140 knots and continue vectoring until you reach the hover stop (eighty-one degrees down-nozzle deflection). In earlier Harriers, because you were entering the

critical area of the envelope at ninety knots, you performed an engine check at this speed to ascertain whether you had sufficient performance to enter vertical flight. With its supercritical wing, which continues to produce lift all the way down to thirty knots, the AV-8B spends far less time in jeopardy, though it is still wise to turn into the wind to avoid the yaw-roll briar patch.

The final deceleration rate is controlled by modulating the nozzle lever from between the hover stop and the braking stop, which is set slightly forward of vertical at 98.5 degrees. Arriving over the intended point of landing at 100 feet, you reduce thrust to pick up a rate of descent while maintaining heading and wing position with reaction controls. As you approach the ground, you have to add just a scootch of power to compensate for the ingestion of hot exhaust, but when you feel the weight on the landing gear, you slam the throttle to idle and unvector the nozzles. All that remains is to shut off the water, engage nosewheel steering, and vacate the pad to make room for your wingman.

Ah, think how good those Gaines-burgers are going to taste.

AV-8B perches atop 23,000 pounds of thrust in a mind-boggling vertical climb.

A huge CH-53E Super Stallion of the HMH 465 "War-horses" settles in at MCASH Tustin, California.

Super Stallion (CH-53)

What has 13,000 horsepower, packs more blades than a Gillette dispenser, and can pick up something its own weight when it gets the urge? Not a clue? Well then, what has three engines, weighs sixteen tons, generates enough static electricity to clear death row in no time flat, and folds down to get on an elevator? One more try? It is capable of handling 93 percent of a Marine division's combat items, retrieving 98 percent of the Marine Corps's aircraft without disassembly, and carrying fifty-five troops 400 miles out for a day in the country and toting them back again when they get bored. The CH-53E. That's right!

Together with its smaller brother the D-model, the Sikorsky Super Stallion provides the Corps with the much needed muscle to transport men and equipment when and where they're most needed. Blessed with tremendous range and good speed (as far as 1,250 nautical miles and up to 170 knots), the Echo allows the Corps to go places and wage war in ways that were inconceivable in the past. It is precisely this flexibility that distinguishes the Marine air/ground team.

There's a lot to get used to with the CH-53s. They're big birds; even when you fold them up, there's no fear of their getting lost. From main ro-

Left: Stallion crew chief signals position of rotor droop stops during pre-flight check out.
Above: CH-53E cruises below KC-130 tanker off Camp Pendleton (note retracted refuelling probe).

tor tip to the arc of the tail rotor, the Echo is nearly eighty feet. That's okay when you're operating from large airfields, but it doesn't hack it aboard ship. Navalizing a bird is not merely a matter of tweaking the metallurgy (though that's an important part); getting it to fit elevators so it can be "struck" below is the real trick—that and getting it to snuggle together with others on the hanger deck when it arrives. Folded, the Echo shrinks to a third of its all-up area, ending up as a twenty-six—by sixty-foot package -small enough that with a little Vaseline it can squeak down the elevator shafts of amphibious assault ships. A lot of ingenuity went into making this happen. The tail boom—driveshaft, rotor, and all—swings counterclockwise to stow along the starboard side of the fuselage, and six of the seven rotors knuckle back like feathers on a bird. The inside is cavernous (thirty feet long and seven-and-a-half feet wide) and capable of handling seven forty- by forty-eight-inch pallets. The amount of stuff that can be shoved aboard is awe-inspiring, but it's the number of people the thing will hold (note the Grenada student evacuation) that's scary. The list of things that "sierra squared" can do is impressive enough, but when you realize that it can be armed with air-to-air missiles and move farther and faster than most other helicopters, you have to consider that it is a quantum advance over its forebears.

The flight deck is separate from the cabin, and you have to climb over a bulkhead to get there. In the cabin, the loadmaster is checking the cargo hook assembly suspended from the main structure above the cabin ceiling, making sure that the support frame and struts are in good shape, that the emergency jettison fitting is rigged, and that the hook operates properly. When deployed, the hook and pendant sling protrude through a hatch in the bottom of the fuselage to a distance of nine feet. For the time being, the gear is stowed with the hatch secured. As HAC (helicopter aircraft commander), you're in the right seat, just the opposite from where you'd sit as pilot in command in a fixed-wing transport but logical because of the location of the rescue hoist on the starboard side adjacent to the forward door. Your mission is to launch forty minutes before sunrise, pick up a 155mm Howitzer on the sling, and take it to an observation post near the FEBA. After the Howitzer has been delivered, you are to retrieve a downed AV-8A and return it to the remote strip for repair. The Harrier pilot had to make an emergency landing after receiving several hits from a dual 23mm AAA battery, electing to set the aircraft down among friendly positions rather than risk losing it to fuel starvation on the way home. It was a wise decision considering that maintenance people and an HST (helicopter support team) had been sent up during the night to prepare the bird for evacuation and it would be only slightly more than half a day before the Harrier was back among its kind undergoing repair.

The Super Stallion's instrument panel is similar to its predecessors, except that with three engines instead of two there's more of everything. Start power is supplied by a self-contained auxiliary power unit, and after all three engines are on the line, the rotors are engaged. It's impressive to watch as the tips of forty-foot blades begin their counterclockwise whirl. Except for the load on the turbines it is inaudible. The blades sweep by faster and faster until they are a blur; it can be hypnotic. There's the strobe effect from the tips, of course, but the sound is absorbing as well. The CH-53 doesn't try to impress you with staccato karate chops; it intimidates you with a menacing growl.

Besides your copilot and yourself, you've got four others: crew chief, loadmaster, and two crewmen outside the aircraft, guiding you through your prelaunch checks. Working the cyclic, you watch as the tracking angle of the rotor changes. With forward stick the rotor head tilts forward and your windscreen fills with blades. Tilted back, just the arc of the tips is visible. At last the checks are completed, and you're ready for flight. In the predawn cool you can expect the bird to want to leap into the air, but by the time you return, you'll be pushing the torque toward the top of the meter.

When they're going up and down, helicopters are really quite logical machines. With zero horizontal velocity, the blades do a complete orbit with a constant bite. The amount of lift that they create is a function of their rotational velocity (a constant in terms of rotor rpm) and pitch (bite). To ascend, you pull up on the collective pitch handle in the cockpit. This tells the blades to take a bigger bite of air, which they try to do. The minute the blades increase their angle of attack on the air, the load on the rotor increases, acting to slow it down. Sensing the slowdown, a servo sends a signal to the engines saying, "Hey guys, send me some more torque." The result of all this madness is an increase in lift, and if this is greater than the weight of the aircraft and its contents, the beast will go up. To hover, you have merely to set the collective at the point at which lift *equals* weight and you'll stay there. Decrease it and you'll descend. This is the way things work as long as the output of the engines is up to the task. If it isn't, you go to the emergency procedures.

In any event, vertical flight makes sense; it's trying to go somewhere with the bird that's absurd. There's probably a swimming analogy somewhere, but try to visualize this: The minute the helicopter picks up a horizontal vector (starts to go from Point A to Point B), the blades on one side are capable of creating more lift than the ones on the other. Say the helicopter is traveling at 120 knots. Viewed from the top, with the rotor spinning counterclockwise, the blades on the right are advancing into a headwind while those on the left are retreating on a tailwind. The difference in wind velocity between the blades at the three o'clock and nine o'clock positions is 240 knots, and that is where the trouble lies. If you did nothing to correct for this, you'd produce so much more lift on the right side that you'd corkscrew uncontrollably to the left until the rotor broke or you hit the ground. Either is unsatisfactory.

What the rotor hub does is compensate for this airspeed differential by constantly varying the pitch of the blades as they track around the circle. They take their smallest bite at the three o'clock position (actually 90 degrees earlier at the twelve o'clock position in conformance with the physical principles of a gyroscope, but there's no sense being quite so technical at this juncture), gradually increasing until half-way around the orbit they are rotated to their greatest angle of attack. The amount of dif-

Above: Stallion's-eye view of harrowing air refuelling.
Below: Aircraft viewed from cargo door of the KC-130 tanker. Note convolutions of the seven-blade rotor at this speed (120 knots).

ferential between the two extremes is a function of airspeed, which brings up a final point about helicopter flight. In a single-rotor system, no matter what you do to delay it, there comes that point beyond which—as on maps of old—"there be dragons." The rotor blade is an airfoil, a wing if you will, and like any wing, it will stall when pushed past its critical angle of attack. The moment of truth arrives when the retreating (nine o'clock) blade can no longer produce enough lift to offset that of the advancing blade, and once it is reached, the aircraft will go immediately and catastrophically out of control and self-destruct. Depending on atmospheric conditions and the aircraft's gross weight, this upper speed limit for the CH-53 is in the vicinity of 170 knots.

Power failures (partial or total) in turbine helicopters are rare in peacetime, yet you spend a lot of your time practicing "autorotations." The reason is that power failure is a lot more prevalent when the enemy starts sending little pieces of metal to compete for airspace. You can sustain a lot of battle damage in a CH-53 and still survive—if your rotors are still there and if (in the event of power loss) you have enough altitude or airspeed to begin with. The procedure for handling an engine failure may seem strange, but it works. Unlike fixed-wing aircraft which lack an affinity for anything less than a well-prepared air base, helicopters have landed in places even mountain goats prefer to avoid and have flown again.

The first thing you do is dump (lower) the collective pitch, that is, decrease the bite of the rotor blades in order to keep the rotor speed up. When everything stabilizes out, this act of maintaining rotor speed translates into some combination of forward airspeed and descent rate, the values of each depending on the amount of power that might still be available and on the weight of the aircraft. While you've got plenty of altitude, you can jockey things around by trading a little height for airspeed (or vice versa), but as you get closer to the ground, your touchdown options begin to shrink rapidly. If conditions permit, you'd like to set things up to arrive a half mile from touchdown at 1,000 feet with 130 knots airspeed. From here you feed in back cyclic to slow, looking to arrive on very short final at 100 feet and 30 knots. At this point you are committed to landing on a particular piece of ground, but by pulling up on the collective, you use the stored energy of the whirling rotor to cushion your descent. By definition, this is a crash, but properly done, it can be a very gentle one.

Enough of this theory and planning for emergencies, let's get this thing into the air! Increasing collective to 60 percent torque, you feel the bird lighten on its gear then unstick. Nothing startling about it, no swaying or protesting; it just goes up with a sort of haughtiness that says, "Look, guys, I'm the king of the wop-wops and don't you forget it." At ten feet you park it and check the engine readings, and when everything looks good you squeeze in more collective and begin your translation to forward flight by pushing forward on the cyclic. There's a moment there when you can feel yourself on the cusp between hover and flight, but it is quickly past and you head for the staging area three miles south, where a crew is waiting with the Howitzer.

Even before you've broken into a hover over the pad, the cargo hook has been deployed and the grounding cable dropped. All helicopters create static electricity, but the Echo takes the cake. With its seven blades churning through the air, the charge that builds up can kill. Until the discharge cable is on the ground, anyone who touches the hook could be subjected to as much as 20,000 volts.

The loadmaster, peering down through the hatch, guides you over the pallet with minute corrections while the HST troops strain against the pounding rotor wash to slip the cables into the hook and lock it shut. The first attempt fails because you drift a little too far to the right, but on the second try everything clicks and you're off. With the Howitzer hanging nearly thirty feet beneath the belly, you ascend to fifty feet before transitioning to horizontal flight. Seventy knots will be your climb and cruise speed for the leg, and though the terrain will be rising steadily beneath you, 2,500 feet will keep you safely above any obstacles.

Like the Delta, the Echo is a joy to fly when everything is working right. Your feet stay on the floor, and it just motors on majestically, seemingly oblivious to the mayhem it's dispensing to the air around it. Left to its own devices, no helicopter likes to fly. They are at war with the elements, which is why so much time has been spent turning the CH-53 into a docile servant. Much of the success in accomplishing this goal is owed to its dual digital flight control systems with their powerful stability augmentation functions, but there's a lot to be said for the elastomeric rotor head and fiberglass-covered blades, which are a far cry from their predecessors. If the stability augmentation systems were to fail, the aircraft could become a handful, but luckily a dual system failure is a rare occurrence.

With an external load slung beneath the aircraft, the bird is maneuverable, a good thing because you're approaching Indian territory. Most of the way to the observation post you have been in the lee of 7,000-foot mountains, but your approach to the drop pad (which is located in a clearing on the east side of the range) is by way of a small valley whose floor is 2,800 feet in elevation. Because the pad is located so close to the cut, wind has been a factor in the past, but this morning it is totally calm, as borne out by the lazy motions of a smoke flare. Off-loading the Howitzer takes seconds. Freed of the millstone, you wheel back through the valley and head for the Harrier.

Defueled and stripped of all externals, the AV-8 still weighs in at a whopping 13,000 pounds. With 8,000 pounds for fuel and crew, the Super Stallion and its cargo will weigh nearly 54,000 pounds—considerably below its maximum capacity, but respectable when you consider the density altitude ratio. The Harrier is parked in a clearing at 2,700 feet above sea level. On what is considered a standard day, the temperature for that elevation should be fifty degrees Fahrenheit, but today it is already nearing eighty degrees. The additional thirty degrees result in a decrease in the air's density, making the helicopter's engines think they are operating at 5,000 feet. Your shaft horsepower is roughly 15 percent less than it would be at sea level on a standard day, and if you waited until noon with the temperature over 100 degrees, your density altitude would be 6,000 feet, sacking your turbines of more than 20 percent of their power.

The Harrier is rigged with a sling that is attached to four predetermined locations. The plan is for you to hover over the load while the loadmaster and helicopter support team grapple the sling with the hook. More so than with a pallet, it is essential for you to come straight up to prevent damage to the Harrier by dragging it across the ground or letting it corkscrew as the wind catches it. While you gain altitude, it will twirl and sway freely, but once you pick up airspeed, the stabilizing chute that has been attached to the Harrier's tail will settle it out.

The clearing is smaller than you expected, with rocks and scruffy juniper trees and thick brambles on all sides. Open to the south, it is fully exposed to an up-slope wind, and you find yourself fighting to keep the aircraft steady as you hover out and lower yourself down to pick up the load.

"Left five feet . . . easy . . . a little more . . . stop."

The loadmaster keeps up a continuous barrage of little instructions to guide you to the hook-up.

"Bring it on down now . . . more . . . more . . . easy . . . whoa!"

The helicopter is bucking and heaving, and you can imagine how it is for the guys who are trying to snap the hook shut.

"You're slewing right . . . bring it back . . . that's right . . . steady . . . steady . . . got it!"

Phew. Now comes the tricky part—you have to center directly over the load and then bring it straight up without shying off to the side. You can feel yourself fencing with the wind, trying to intuit its rhythm, and when you know you can't delay another instant, you pull the collective up smoothly but firmly, feeling the hook accept the load and haul it free. The load starts to oscillate, side to side at first, then in circles as it catches the rotor wash. Finally you're high enough to add forward cyclic, and almost immediately the drag chute grabs and the oscillation stops.

Special squadron HMX-1 provides executive helo transport for the president and other top government leaders.

Huey (UH-1N)

Until February 1964, when the first Huey arrived, MCAS(H) New River was the rock-ribbed bastion of the piston-thumping, fire-belching, bolt-shuddering H-34, the mainstay of the utility helicopter world. Like Chevy's answer to Ford's immortal flathead V-8—long-standing king of the hot-rodding hill—the first UH-1E roared in from the west and the contest was over before its blades stopped. The Sikorsky Seahorse was dethroned, pounded into extinction by an aircraft with half as many blades, whose repertoire of unworldly noises has become its hallmark, one that troops the world over have come to respect. Purists no doubt shuddered at the indignity of having to assault the upper reaches without becoming arthritic rotating the twist grip on the collective pitch (torque control) handle—indeed there are still diehards around who mourn the Sikorsky sky-stomper's demise twenty years later—but the Huey became to Marine rotary aviation what the Hercules was to the fixed-wingers: A workhorse whose reliability and ruggedness took much of the mystery out of the business.

The bird was christened Iroquois, but the name never stuck. Its initial designation when it entered service with the Army in 1959 was HU-1, but long before the letters were reversed, its familiar name was legitimized by the manufacturer who distinguished one directional pedal from the other by embossing the name "Bell" on the right and "Huey" on the left. The first model sported 770 shaft horsepower, a payload of 3,200 pounds, a fully loaded cruise speed of 60 knots, and a range of over 160 nautical miles. At a reduced loading, the cruise speed rose to over 100 knots, but it was clear almost immediately that it needed more power. The follow-on UH-1B (basis for the Corps's UH-1E) had 1,100 horsepower, giving it a nearly 4,000-pound payload, a 225-mile range, and cruise speeds of between 95 and 120 knots, depending on weight. With a crew of three (two pilots and a crew chief)

Recon grunts rappel from a UH-1N Huey at El Toro Air Show.

it could carry six passengers or be configured with a variety of weapons, many of which just sort of appeared in the field after a little judicious cluging.

The UH-1E was a navalized B-model, having different radios, rotor brake, personnel hoist, and a larger rotor to give it greater lifting capacity. Though it is identical in shape, the airframe is heavier than that of the Army's because it is made of aluminum rather than magnesium, which would be eaten to bits by the salt spray attending carrier operations. A less obvious (but hardly trivial) by-product of this material change was that Echos were less apt to burn than magnesium aircraft, and when they did catch fire, they took longer to consume and burned with less intensity.

Huey's significance was not just that it could fly farther, faster, and with more payload than the air-craft it supplanted, nor even that it was more rug-ged, more reliable, more maintainable, and able to sustain incredible amounts of battle damage and live to fight another day. It was all of these plus the bonus that because it was easier to fly, it took less time to train a pilot to fly one than it did a piston-pounder, allowing the Corps to close the helicopter aviator supply-versus-demand gap far more rapidly than would ever have been possible with the H-34.

As was the case of the Phantom on the fixed-wing side, the UH-1E went on to become *the* wop-wop of the Vietnam War, performing such incred-ible feats that even its designers must reflect on their accomplishment with a certain amount of awe. The UH-1N entered service with the Corps in 1972, taking up the standard without a bobble, and it has remained the utility workhorse clear to the present. With its twin turbine power packs coupled, the ship has 1,290 shaft horsepower available for takeoff, but if either engine has to be shut down, a governor in the fuel control is bypassed, giving the pilot ac-cess to 800 horsepower from the remaining engine. The N-model can carry a thousand pounds more load than the Echo nearly ninety miles farther. It is even more rugged than its predecessor and can pack double the number of passengers.

Huey over Twentynine Palms desert sports cylindrical "ballroom mirror" to confuse infrared-seeking missiles.

Most days in combat start early, and this one's no exception with a 0430 launch to insert a ten-man recon patrol. It meant a 0200 wake-up for a 0230 brief in the battalion ops tent. By the crow-fly the hop from the battalion area to the landing zone is only a twelve-mile shot, but by the time you skirted the hills to enter the LZ from the south, the flight had covered nearly forty miles. The LZ is a boulder-strewn plateau 2,500 feet above the valley floor. There was no thought of touching down in the dark, but by using night vision goggles to position yourself, you were able to hover at fifteen feet, discharging the team one at a time to rappel to the ground. Departing at ten-second intervals, it had taken the troops nearly two minutes to clear the aircraft -a long time when you're over someone else's turf—but the insertion was without incident, and the aircraft was back on the ground before first light. It was nice to return for a little chow, even if it was SOS (if you don't know, don't ask) flushed

115

down with battery-acid coffee, but you had barely sat down with your mess kit when the call came to get back to the ops tent, where you learned that the recon team had run into an ambush.

Now it's 0550, twenty minutes to sunrise, and your heart is pounding from the quarter-mile run from ops to the helo pad. Ordnance men are swarming over the aircraft as you shimmy into the seat and hit the battery, master, and start switches even before strapping in. Your copilot, who stayed behind to copy frequencies, is still a hundred yards away as the engine lights, and the rotor is almost up to speed before he has strapped himself in and attached his mike and headset cords. Still panting, he sketches the situation.

"We're to contact Nestor Two-Two on Fox Mike [FM radio frequency]. They're being pounded by mortars. Four WIAs . . . two serious. They're rearming a section of Harriers with Rockeyes and diverting a Bronco and some Cobras, but it'll be twenty minutes before they all arrive. We're it until then."

The aircraft had been unarmed for the insertion, but now seven-shot rocket pods of 2.75-inch rockets are mounted on the aft landing-skid braces on either side of the aircraft, and an M-60 machine gun rests on its free mount in the doorway. If necessary, it can be pitched out to make room, but for the time being it's comforting to know that it's there.

Normally, a series of ground checks is carried out in conjunction with the ground crew, but because this is an emergency scramble and because the controls were checked on the earlier flight, it is skipped. Instrument readings are in the green, so with a thumbs-up to the lineman and a look back to make sure that the crew chief is ready, you haul up on the collective to get airborne and almost immediately feed in forward cyclic to accelerate away before banking hard right toward the east. No forty-mile runaround this time. Surprise is out, so you point for the saddle in the hills ten miles east and let her rip. With pods and a gun, the Huey is no

speed burner. You're lucky to get ninety-five knots in a cruise climb, but still you'll be over the action in less than ten minutes—fifteen since you left the mess hall. As you clear the hill and dive into the valley, you don't need a map to tell you where the friendlies are. Their position is marked by dust and smoke as livid explosions heave geysers of flame and dirt fifty feet into the air. With all the noise and confusion, you might think your presence would go unnoticed, but no sooner have you crossed the ridgeline than your FM radio comes alive.

"This is Nestor Two-Two. This is Nestor Two-Two. How do you read, over?"

"Five-by-five, Nestor Two-Two," he answers, acknowledging first-rate communications. "This is Chariot. How me?"

"I read you the same. We can't see the mortars, but we're getting pretty heavy small-arms fire from the tree line 500 meters north and slightly above us. Do you have them?"

"Negative, Two-Two, we're still too far away. What's your situation?"

It's not good at all. They've taken another casualty and they're pinned down in the open without a sheltered escape route. Meanwhile, the enemy is advancing under the concealment of a stand of trees: It's just a matter of time before they will be in position to take the team under direct fire. There can be no thought of dashing in and extricating the team for the time being. It would be suicide to try until the mortars have been silenced and the enemy troops taken under fire. There's another consideration. You're clattering around in Indian country, and that makes you a big fat target yourself. The small arms fire is probably not a great threat, and the ruggedness of the terrain tends to rule out triple-A, but you take nothing for granted. It's the likely presence of SAM-7, hand-held, heat seeking missiles that's the real danger. The key is to get down low, keep moving, and look for every little piece of terrain that can mask you for even a second.

"Chariot, this is Cowboy, an OV-10 three min-

utes out with a pair of Cobras ten miles in trail. What's the situation?"

Quickly a plan forms. With its greater speed and firepower, the OV-10 is a much better aircraft to hunt up the mortars and coordinate the extraction. With their 20mm cannon, the Cobras can beat up the tree line while the Harriers take on the mortars once they've been located. While that's going on, it'll be your job to dash in and extract the team. Here again it's the coordination that is important. It's daylight now, so even it you can't find a place to touch down, you should be able to hover low enough for the wounded to be stowed in the cabin before the rest of the team clambers aboard. With any luck, the whole sequence will take less than a minute, and though it is highly unlikely that all of the mortars will be taken out, the shock of the air strike should silence them long enough for you to do your job.

The Cobras and Harriers (Fang and Zipper flights) have checked in with Cowboy during the time it has taken you to traverse the area south of the LZ and wheel back around to the north, staying well clear of the tree line. Your course is a series of jinks in both altitude and heading, and your senses are fine-tuned in anticipation of the ground fire that

Troop-carrying Hueys line up at the Twentynine Palms airfield fuel pumps.

will come sooner or later. Then for a mile off to the right at two o'clock, you catch a glimpse of motion just below a massive rock outcrop. The mortars.

"Cowboy, this is Chariot. I think I got the mortars. They're about a click and a half north of the friendlies. Do you want me to mark?"

"Affirmative, Chariot. Give me about thirty seconds to get into position."

There's just a fixed sight, but it doesn't matter. You're going to let a pack go at long range in an arc—not a terribly accurate maneuver, but good enough for referencing.

"Chariot in hot."

"You're cleared."

You've worked around until you're north and west of the clearing, hugging the deck to remain out of view, but now you wheel the aircraft around in a tight right turn, steady up on line, and when it feels right, rock the nose back and let fly. Instantly a salvo of rockets erupts from the right-hand pod, rippling past on a shimmering wake. It's an odd sight. Unlike Zunis (five-inch rockets), 2.75s don't go straight: They corkscrew their way along a general flight path. It's because their stabilizing fins are recessed, not fixed, ready to pop out at launch. It's a rare case in which all the fins come out together and in perfect alignment: As usual, all wobble around, and one seems to be doing barrel rolls around the rest as they pass their zenith and curve back toward earth. Even before they've hit the ground, you've sheared away to the west, and just as you begin your reverse to the south, they impact, neatly bracketing the area.

"Roger the spot," confirms Cowboy. A little later he adds, "That's where they are."

This is where it all comes together. The Cobras are orbiting in the clear, southeast of the friendly position. You're heading back along the tree line ready to make your dash. The Harriers are poised to strike, awaiting the OV-10's marking run. They've got four Rockeye pods (canisters containing hundreds of explosive submunitions that break open in midair) apiece, which will mow down anyone or anything in the open over an enormous area with lethal projectiles. The recon team is standing by with smoke ready to mark the LZ, and your crew chief has stowed the machine gun so it won't obstruct the doorway. When the retraction goes, it goes at full volume.

"Cowboy in for a marking run."

"I've got your smoke. Zipper's thirty seconds from target."

"Roger, you're cleared. Hit my smoke."

"Fang's commencing attack. We're a minute out from the tree line."

"Chariot's inbound. Give me some smoke." With a flick of left cyclic, you're rolling back around to the LZ.

Red smoke boils out of the rocks, showing a wind from the south. There's a small ledge ten feet this side of the smoke that is too small to land on, but it should allow you to set your right skid down while the team gets aboard. Your copilot unstraps

and climbs back into the cabin to lend a hand in the boarding operation as you break the aircraft into a hover and slide sideways the last twenty feet to the ledge before lowering gently onto the rock. Even before contact, your crew chief is out of the aircraft, directing the litter bearers around the front of the chopper to the open hatch. As a second litter is muscled up onto the rock, he takes an end from a Marine whose leg is bandaged and guides it up into the cabin. Three more wounded are helped aboard and the rest of the team, heads low in the maelstrom, arrives on the run. When the last is aboard, the crew chief throws a thumbs-up and dives through the hatch. With the gusting wind and constantly changing weight and center of gravity, you've had to make thousands of minute corrections with collective, cyclic, and directional pedals. You've made them subconsciously, concentrating on the situation around you. At first there was no reaction, but then sporadic patches of small arms rounds started whizzing around the chopper, boring high-pitched holes in the empty air. Then all at once the volume of fire soars, and the bird is hammered by a rapid series of bangs. A hundred meters away, there's a crash of thunder as a mortar round slams into a rock wall. You pull collective to the stop, and before you're clear enough to bank away to the south, you feel, more than hear, the staccato rap of another burst of fire finding its mark.

"Chariot's outbound, clearing the area to the south."

"Roger Chariot, cleared to Wayside. Break. Break. Fang flight, break it off to the east."

In the back, the copilot and the crew chief are tending to the wounded while the rest of the team lies sprawled on the decking in total exhaustion. As you climb back out of the valley you emerge suddenly from the shadow of the hills and into the blinding sunlight. For a moment you're confused, shocked that it's still early morning. Maybe it's that you feel a little older than you did when you launched.

Sea Cobra (AH-1)

When it's time to get down and dirty in the mud, the first ones there are the Cobras. Clattering into the LZ at the head of the parade, they can hug the sagebrush and peer into gopher burrows. Able to flow with the landscape, the snakes are nimble, durable, and when the time comes, deadly. They are the kind of bird that ground troops lust after. Everybody wants more of them except (it seems) the people who authorize their procurement. Although Marines would like more of all inventory aircraft, the AH-1 leads the list.

There are three versions of the Cobra, and they are quite distinct, showing an evolving philosophy in the role of attack helicopters in the post-Vietnam battlefield. The AH-1J was the Corps's first venture into the attack helicopter field. Thirty-eight AH-1Gs had been procured in 1969 for training and initial operations pending receipt of the J-model, which differed from the Army's AH-1G primarily in powerplant (twin engine versus one), armament (20mm three-barrel cannon versus 7.62mm guns),

and a variety of navalization features. The last two AH-1J airframes were modified to become prototypes for the AH-1T, which features upgraded powerplants, increased payload and/or performance potential, and provisions for mounting TOW missiles. Now the AH-1T(Plus) incorporates still more powerful engines, better displays, and provisions for mounting and firing Hellfire missiles. All Cobras have been configured to hang Sidewinder missiles.

Attack helicopters really came into their own with the Huey gunships in Vietnam, and after folks found out how good these were, the program grew like Topsy. At first they were used to engage light targets in and around the LZs, but by the early seventies, the situation was in almost constant flux. The targets were heavier, and Cobras found themselves confronted with bunkers or armor that were too hard for their weaponry. (Toward the end, when enemy tanks were streaming toward Saigon, the Army tested out their TOW-equipped Cobras, scoring numerous hits.) Because of their success in suppressing enemy ground fire during troop in-

sertion, demand for gunships continued to rise. What the ground troops had found was that unless targets could be accurately identified and marked, fixed-wing attack planes were unable to provide the kind of support they needed during assault.

Army and Marine utilization of Cobras remained quite similar for the duration of the war, but since then their programs have diverged. While they still have troop support responsibilities, increasingly the Army's Cobras are being thought of as an antiarmor weapon. The Corps's Cobras are equipped with TOW and Hellfire, but the emphasis of the program is LZ prep and CAS, a direction underscored by the Grenada operation, in which TOW missiles were fired into gun emplacements located in buildings -not the most cost-effective use of the missile unless you value the lives of your buddies as much as the Marines do.

It seems inevitable that night and foul weather troop insertions will become the rule rather than the exception, increasing all the more the importance of the Cobra in matters of LZ reconnaissance and preparation. If enemy fire is encountered during the early stages of an assault, bringing in fixed-wing CAS is almost out of the question until things are sorted out and the exotic target-designating systems are deployed. What this means is that the Cobras are going to have to hold the fort during the early stages of the assault, or until the fixed-wingers can see well enough to separate the good guys from the bad.

Below: TOW anti-tank missile streaks from AH-1T Sea Cobra toward an island target off the California coast.
Right: Two-man Sea Cobra crew of HMA-169, Camp Pendleton. Bird carries full load of eight TOW missiles.

The rear seat of the Cobra is roomy, with outstanding sideways visibility and adequate vision to the front. Because its instrumentation is more complete and because it is considerably roomier, the rear seat is generally occupied by the HAC, but this is not necessarily so. Things are different when you're perched out there in the shark snoot, in a nest that only an A-4 driver could relate to. Down and to the side, the visibility is terrific. Straight ahead, the TOW sight gets in the way, particularly with your view of the flight instruments, but all in all the vantage point is the best there is in aviation. Out there on the front end, you feel like a part of the surrounding terrain. If you're concentrating, anything that moves will get your attention. It's like having a front-row balcony seat for the war, only in this production you get to play a starring role at the same time.

Outfitted for combat, you're wearing the new lightweight body armor, cartridge belt, pistol, canteens, and a host of other grunt-type gear—were it not for your flightsuit and helmet, you could well be mistaken for your mud brothers. It's not by accident. Because even in peacetime, helicopter pilots spend so much time in the field with the grunts, they have developed a bond, which achieves its greatest strength in the Huey and Cobra circles. No place is this more evident than in MAG-39 at Camp Pendleton, where away from the flight line, everyone wears camouflaged utilities. The only way to distinguish between zoomies and grunts is to look for the little pair of gold wings.

For most aviators, the helmet is a brain bucket capable of holding a pair of earphones, a microphone, and a visor in some rough semblance of formation with the crew member's gray-matter. Not so the Cobra pilot, to whom the fit of the helmet is critical. To begin with, you're attached by linkage to the chin-mounted cannon pod. A rod butts up to a fitting on top of your helmet so that when you move your head from side to side or up and down, the motion is transmitted through linkages

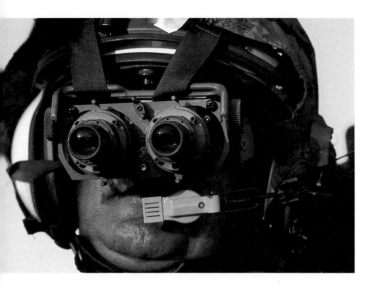

to a control box and thence to the pod. All is well as long as everything stays in alignment, but if your head were free to slosh around in the bucket, you can imagine the thrills you could provide to the friendlies. As you sight through an aiming reticule suspended from your helmet in front of your left eye, the guns follow your movement, so all you have to do is acquire the target with the gun-slew engaged and pull the trigger. You can feel the slight resistance to your head movement, but after a while you accept it and go on about your business.

As if that weren't enough of a load for the helmet, there's the addition of the night vision goggles (NVGs). Years ago, there was a sci-fi movie in which this fishlike creature ran around New York, scaring milk-white virgins on their way home from the malt shop. It wasn't his slimy green scales or his webbed feet and hands that caused all the panic: It was this pair of telescoped eyeballs protruding above his foundered piscine cheeks that evoked the bulk of the terror. But horrible-looking or not, the goggles are stupendous, amplifying ambient light to the point where, on a moonlit night, objects stand out as brightly as they do in full daylight. Up until

the moment you put them on for real and launch out into the dark, you're skeptical—which is as it should be. But as you overcome your initial desire to tear them off (or pluck your eyeballs out) and begin to relax into them, you begin to marvel at how much you can see.

They are not without faults, however. Each new generation of night goggles is lighter, but it is probably fair to say that their weight will never be a trivial problem: To counterbalance them you have to strap lead to the back of your helmet to keep your forehead out of your lap. Another drawback is that your field of vision is narrowed to forty degrees, so you have to develop the habit of turning your whole head up and down as well as from side to side, instead of just moving your eyes. You get used to them after a lot of neck strain, and eventually you become pretty good at using them, as long as you remember that you have no depth perception and that the whole world becomes black and green. Looking inside the cockpit is something of a problem. You have to tilt your head up to look beneath the glasses, and unless you've got white (or blue) lighting, you're going to have trouble reading the gauges because you've blown your dark adaptation. Like most things that allow you to beat nature, the goggles are a trade-off, but one so vastly weighted in your favor they are like a gift from the gods.

Tonight's mission is a troop insert, and it's your job to take your T-model into the LZ just before the Frogs (CH-46s) arrive and, after checking the area out, to stand by to provide suppressive fire if enemy troops are present. Compared to the AH-1J, the Tango is a bit of a dog. The designers more than offset the 250 shaft horsepower increase with 1,400 pounds of added weight. The result is a jump in payload and fighting capacity, but at the cost of some speed and performance. The engine upgrade in the T-Plus cures the problem, but it will be a while before enough of them are in the fleet to make a real difference.

You can fly the bird from either cockpit, but the main flight instrumentation is in the rear. The guy up front is the shooter, since he's able not only to slew the machine gun pods, but guide the TOW missile to the target as well. The way you work the system is to line up the cross hairs on the TOW sight over the target and fire the missile. It's going to head for wherever the cross hairs are pointed, so if you let them drift off, the missile goes somewhere else. It's an extremely accurate missile, but you have to stay with it until impact.

The M-197 three-barreled 20mm cannon pod is a real winner. It carries 750 rounds with a rate of fire of 750 rounds per minute but limited to bursts of sixteen seconds maximum. The gun can be swiveled 110 degrees either side of the nose and elevated up and down 18 and 50 degrees respectively. The beauty is that you control its train angle by turning your head. The hummer just tracks where you look. Look at the target and pull the trigger—

simple as that. For tonight's mission—preceding a flight of CH-46s taking a rifle company into an LZ on the floor of a valley—in addition to the cannon, you're configured with two nineteen shot 2.75-inch rocket packs and two TOWs, so you'll have lots of goodies if things heat up.

You and your wingman have lit off engines in concert with a second section of gunships tasked with escorting the troop transports en route to the LZ, but since they'll proceed by a different route, you'll depart separately. After completing the poststart checks and establishing contact with the rest of the flight, you call for and receive taxi and takeoff clearance. Taxiing a Cobra is a matter of pulling in collective to break ground and then reducing torque until the aircraft is in a low hover between five and ten feet. After scanning the instruments, you ease in lateral cyclic to clear the parking spot, and when you reach the taxiway, you feed forward cyclic to head to the runway. If the pilot in the rear cockpit were in control, he would probably cock the aircraft off one way or the other to get a better view of the taxiway. (It is interesting

---

T-model Sea Cobra carries FLIR (forward-looking infrared) sensor for night and low-visibility operations. Three-barrel 20mm gun magically follows helmet-mounted sight (see previous page).

to watch a flight of Cobras sidling down the taxi-way, each with a different crank to the direction of movement.) On the runway, takeoff is a matter of adding collective while lowering the nose, and allowing the aircraft to accelerate until it has adequate translational lift to commence a climb. Once clear of the field, you pick up your initial heading, check your instruments, and scrunch around to make sure your wingman is in position, forty-five degrees out to your right, 800 feet aft, and stepped slightly up. For most people, this night would be a sea of dim shapes undulating in and out of focus in the pale light of the waning moon, but for you, it is a world of startling green of varying values. The southwest hillsides stand out brilliantly against the black horizon. The lee shadows of rocks and vegetation leap into view without the slightest hint of perspective. Only the relative size of objects gives a clue as to their proximity. Orientation is a matter of aggregating impressions gained from a hundred known objects and constructing from these what to you is a rational and coherent universe in which real boundaries have been left behind.

You're faster, but not a lot faster, than the CH-46s, so you and your wingman will take off slightly earlier and proceed separately to the LZ while a

second section of Cobras escorts the transports. Two more sections of Cobras are standing strip-alert at the field, and a Bronco will be overhead, coordinating the insertion. The LZ has been selected to allow friendly artillery to range the area while masking it from the enemy's heavy guns. The intelligence briefer estimated that the nearest enemy troops were seven miles north of the LZ and that even if they had moved south (an unlikely event since they had spent the day digging in), it was doubtful that they could be within two miles at the time of the insertion. Sitting there while the aircraft is firing up, you're visualizing the LZ with its flat basin flanked by broad slopes leading up to rocky spiked hills. The bottom of the basin is really a dry lake bed whose center is still wet from a recent barrage of thunderstorms, but that's not where the LZ is. It's at the very edge in the lee of the eastern hills, close enough to where the troops can find cover and concealment in the sharply etched runoff channels that crease the gradual slope. The last several troop insertions have gone without incident, but you learn to take optimistic appraisals from intelligence with a grain of salt. It's much better to prepare for the worst and let the surprises be nice ones.

Airborne, the Cobra is . . . nifty. It steps out and cruises without a lot of fuss and bother, bites smoothly into turns, and holds straight and level without protest. At first, you have problems keeping it in balanced flight, particularly in the front cockpit where the flight instruments are obscured by the TOW sight. When it goes into its combat mode, the Cobra struts its stuff. It'll wheel and turn and dive with the best of them, pull off, and be back on target so quickly it'll make you wet your pants if you're the guy on the ground it's going after. Stick responsiveness in the front cockpit (the control pole sits off to the side on the right console as it does in the F-16) is four times greater than in the rear, so it takes a little finesse at first. Even with the cannon fixed in the straight-ahead mode,

124

you can bring the weapons to bear with incredible speed. The one thing you can't do is unload it to negative g. The phenomenon is called "mast bumping," and it occurs when the blades, creating lift in the opposite (wrong) direction, deflect and strike the aircraft. It's a no-no because without its rotor, the Cobra ceases flight abruptly and not always with your best interests at heart.

"Wolfman, this is Swamp Pup on Fox Mike, over." The OV-10 is airborne and looking for you on the FM radio.

"Roger, Swamp Pup. Wolfman is orbiting Golf awaiting the push."

"Okay, Wolfman. The Frogs are three miles out. Stand by to push."

You check that the armament switches are set for firing twenty mike-mike (20mm), and you slew the barrels to their full limits to check that every-

thing is working. It will take three minutes to get to the LZ after the push, which will give you two minutes to poop and snoop the area. The critical time is when the first section of Frogs is on the ground getting ready to lift and the second is breaking into hover. If they get hit with heavy ground fire at that moment, the insertion could turn into a disaster with no choice but to continue with the mission.

"Okay, Wolfman. Go to it."

Your wingman drops back in trail as you round the corner of the western hills and turn north into the valley. The ground below is deeply etched by what was once a raging river. Ahead the valley broadens, and by following the gently slumping shoulders to the floor, you pick out the playa and the LZ along the eastern edge. The straps bite into your shoulders as you press forward to see. The flight comes in quickly, zigzagging out of sync at fifty feet. The threat—if indeed there is any—is off to the east of the LZ, where a regiment could be hidden in the gullies, so you concentrate on the flanks of the hills. As the lead division of transports enters the zone, you pass them abeam and slide around behind them. They're touching down, and you watch as troops come streaming out of the four choppers, fanning out as they head for the hillside. You're back in front of them as the lead chopper lifts. You hold your breath. "Does it come now?" you wonder, but the others follow quickly and the zone is clear for the second division.

Blap! A flare ignites above the LZ turning night to day and searing your eyes through the goggles. You turn away quickly, but not before you see the eruption of a mortar round not twenty feet from a hovering transport. Your Cobra banks hard to the right away from the LZ and toward the mountains, which are alive with ground fire. The aircraft is vibrating wildly as you skim the slope, racing to lay down covering fire. "Are we hit?" you wonder, and then you realize that it's the recoil from your gun that's socking the airframe.

"This is Knee Deep Two-Dash-Two. We're hit and shutting down. There's a pot full of casualties down here, so we'll need a medevac bird." Another flare goes off, and the pounding by the mortars increases. Ground fire continues to come from the hillside, although as your wingman makes his pass, its volume diminishes noticeably.

"Center the gun and we'll let them have it with the rockets." The third wave is about to land. Though the rockets are not necessarily more effective than the cannon, they will get their attention better.

The Cobra bores in from the west, waiting until the slant range is less than a thousand feet before salvoing a rocket pod. Erupting from their nest beneath the port stub wing, the rockets blaze away with a muted roar, scorching your already tender eyes. The hillside blossoms with explosions as you wheel away, but not before you've released the cannon and cut loose again.

The escort Cobras arrive with the last division, and as their wards touch down, they shear away and join in laying down suppressive fire. It's manic. You've been here less than eight minutes— five since the firing began—but you've lost all track of time. It could have been ten seconds for all you know, but you get some kind of indication when you realize that the cannon has run out of ammunition. Stowing the gun in its forward position, you reset the switches to fire your TOW missiles. It's hardly a worthy target for such an expensive weapon, but you have to do something to take some of the pressure off the LZ.

The last of the transports leaves the area, having picked up the crew and wounded from the downed Frog. The mortars have yet to be found, but now that the troops have taken cover in the gullies, they are of less concern. Robbed of lucrative targets, enemy ground fire has dropped away to nothing. One pass along the silent hillside and then another. Nothing. Less than five minutes of on-station time remains, and you strain to find a target, without success. Then on the very last sweep a 23mm gun opens up, and you mark its location.

"Ten o'clock slightly low for one click." You toggle the intercom with your right heel, grab for the straps to release the goggles, and rock forward to use the TOW sight. Even before you've finished talking, the Cobra sheers sixty degrees left—so close to being on target that it takes just a small correction for you to lay the cross hairs over the gun position.

Whoosh! One TOW is away, tracking down the line between you and the target. No sooner has the first missile crumped into the hillside than the sec-

AH-1T Sea Cobra can carry an awesome array of ordnance—20 mm cannon, rockets, TOW missiles, bombs, and more, to the modern battlefield.

ond is away in hot pursuit. Again there is a bright flash followed by a shower of sparks. The gun remains silent as you wingover back around. Goggles back in place again, you scan the area, but nothing is moving, and you figure one of the two missiles had to get the gunner unless you completely lost sight of the emplacement.

"Wolfman lead is Winchester." You inform Swamp Pup and your wingman that you're out of ammo. "Let's head for the barn."

Bronco (OV-10)

It looks like it evolved from something out of a primeval forest. Its straight, stubby wings allow a pair of elongated engine nacelles to fly loose wing on an extruded CONEX box, while at the back the high-flying tail plane pins things together so that the whole assemblage doesn't fall apart. At a glance you know that it has a sinister intent, and loaded for bear it looks downright evil.

The Bronco began life as the Marine Corps's LARA (light armed reconnaissance aircraft), destined for duty in Vietnam as a FAC and helicopter escort bird. In the ensuing years it has evolved into quite an impressive aircraft with specialties not found anywhere else in the Corps. There are two variants, the Alpha and Delta, each with its own set of capabilities. Both are two-seaters in a tandem configuration, equipped with sponson-mounted hardpoints for carrying a variety of fixed-firing and release stores. Both have HF and UHF radios, which allow the pilot and his AO (aerial observer)—a ground officer (often a cannon-cocker) trained for the task at MCAS(H) New River—to talk to nearly everyone, making the Bronco an indispensable asset in virtually any tactical situation. While it is commonly thought of as a TACA/FACA aircraft, it is much more. Often it provides communications linkage with disparate elements of a command, adjusting naval gunfire and artillery to coincide with ground maneuvers and air strikes. Forward maneuvering element commanders count on Broncos to keep them abreast of friendly as well as enemy unit locations and to relay instructions when terrain masking is a factor.

You may not have suspected it, but the Bronco can act as a transport. The area behind the rear cockpit can hold up to five people and, in the case of the Alpha, can be used for paradrops. The rear fairing can be removed, allowing for static line drops at low or high altitude. (It is also possible with the Delta, except that its door holds a bunch of electronic equipment, so removing it not only sacks some of the aircraft's potential, but inasmuch as it weighs nearly 500 pounds, it poses a handling problem as well.) One method used for the clandestine insertion of recon elements has the Bronco charging in at 200 feet and 200 knots, pulling up into the vertical, and excreting the jumpers (with or without their consent) at 400 to 600 feet. It's an exciting act and one that offers far more secrecy and security than either a helo insert or high-altitude jump from a KC-130.

What's back there is what makes the D-model special—the goodies for the LST, FLIR, and automatic video tracker. With that little ball under the nose of the Delta, the pilot or AO is able to designate a target and have the system stay on it as long as it remains within the gimbal limits of the tracker. The system can provide the pilot with release information for his own use or can illuminate the target for other aircraft equipped to acquire a laser return. In a field trial the belly of a Delta was carved up to carry a three-barrel 20mm M-197 cannon pod light-fingered out of a Cobra. This was hooked to the spot tracker so that when the AO designated a target, it was brought under extremely accurate fire automatically, a fact confirmed on video tapes of numerous day and night runs.

To accommodate communications with ground units without radios, the AO has a small hatch in the floor (grenade hole), through which he can deliver Polaroid pictures and/or messages to the folks on the ground. Message drop delivery is simplicity itself. The pilot descends to treetop level at 200 knots, and as the target passes under the Pitot tube on the nose, he counts to three and instructs the AO to let loose the weighted leather pouch. More than one grunt has been stunned (literally) by the accuracy of the maneuver.

It is as if the Bronco is the repository of all the techniques of the past that have seemingly been rendered obsolete in the modern battlefield. Every field commander will tell you that it is right in the thick of battle that high-tech is most apt to become unglued, and that's where the Bronco comes to the fore. Sure, a helicopter could do the job, but not as well. What the Bronco has going for it is survivability. With its modified exhaust ducts, it has the lowest IR signature of all Marine tactical aircraft. Moreover, it is equipped with chaff and flare dispensers to help it defeat radar and heat-seeking missiles. It is nearly twice as fast as the fastest helicopters, allowing it to maneuver clear of danger while increasing its coverage of the battle area. It is more maneuverable than any fixed-wing it is liable to meet, and able to make darting attacks on enemy helicopters that allow it to bring its own weapons to bear without entering into the range of their missiles. In a burst of insight, the planners equipped both the Alpha and Delta with provisions for hanging a Sidewinder air-to-air missile under each wing. Native ability notwithstanding, the primary advantage of the Bronco lies in the tactics Marines employ, such as staying below 300 feet while darting in and out of masking terrain.

SEAD (as in "see ad") stands for suppression of enemy air defenses and is one of the many techniques developed to help aircraft survive in a tactical environment. Anytime you're facing enemy troops, it has application, and tonight is no exception. During the briefing, you talk easily about it, as if it were a snap. It isn't. The idea is to employ every weapon at your disposal to help the attack aircraft get in and out of the target without getting tagged. Sometimes this means engaging radar facilities or missile launchers, but in a front-line battlefield situation, this generally comes down to getting the attention of the people with the shoulder-mounted heat-seeking missiles and making them keep their heads down while the fast-movers do their thing. In the normal division of labor, your job as pilot will be to coordinate with the attack aircraft while the AO deals with the ground units, particularly "Arty," or naval gunfire, if it's available. Often it doesn't take much, and even when the enemy troops are in defilade, air-detonated fire can be effective. Anything that diverts attention from the attacking aircraft is valuable, and in some cases it is worthwhile having artillery fire striking the target in concert with the aircraft.

Right: VMO-2 Bronco driver Lt. Dave ''Cow'' Gurney debriefs mission during summer maneuvers at Twenty-nine Palms.

Below: Highly maneuverable OV-10 plunges like a prehistoric bird of prey toward the desert floor.

Three-man recon team is literally dumped from the rear compartment of an A-model Bronco. Plane roars in at treetop level, pitches vertically, and drops its human cargo at 800 feet.

It's a "routine" situation, which is to say that you'll be working the area around the FEBA, waiting for things to turn to worms. During the day, two companies have been on the move, meeting token resistance along their route of advance on a mile-wide front. Just prior to nightfall, they deployed in a hasty defense, awaiting daybreak before continuing on to their objective at the north end of the valley. Your job is to maintain contact while lying in readiness, spring-loaded to respond should trouble occur. Hanging out waiting for trouble to start seems to be your daily fare.

On the taxi out, your AO adjusts the FLIR, presenting you with an infrared image on the repeater display on your forward panel. "Hot" objects can be shown either lighter or darker than "cold" objects, as desired. Though most people tend to visualize "hot" with lighter colors, there are circumstances in which the opposite offers better enhancement. Mostly it is preference, and yours conforms to the mainstream.

The OV-10 was designated to work off unimproved strips, so the overstuffed landing gear handles the dips and depressions of the roadway without trouble. Catching a right-angle gust as it clears the top of the tree line, the aircraft yaws precipitously to the right, feeling for an instant as if it were ready to teeter over a hidden brink, then finding its footing again, it rights itself in a solid stance and muscles its way into the sky. It is 0445, ninety minutes to first light and two hours until you're back on the deck. There's enough left of the moon to bathe the terrain in a soft blue-gray monochrome wash, the deeper tucks and folds standing out in undulating relief. The moon and stars are fuzzy, cloaked in a mantle of dust sucked into the tropopause by storm-driven winds 500 miles to the west and borne on the easterly flow en route to the steppes of Asia. It's a milk-bowl effect that sometimes makes it difficult to maintain orientation without reference to your attitude instruments. It's quiet at the front, with just an occasional pop of

A remarkably versatile aircraft, the Bronco is successfully used by the Marines in battlefield observation, anti-helicopter, and light-attack roles.

an illumination round to witness the presence of man.

"Lampshade to Argon. Lampshade to Argon. Come in please." The Fox Mike comes alive, and despite the severe frequency clipping, there is an unmistakable urgency in the hushed voice. Involuntarily you will Argon onto the net.

"Go ahead, Lampshade, this is Argon." Dispassionate . . . remote . . . detached. You envision someone in the midst of a game of acey-deucy pausing to respond before laying waste to his opponent's unprotected men.

"I have movement in front of me on the other side of the spur. It's . . . "

The night erupts in a cataclysm of mortar fire.

From the air the assault appears as a dizzying array of photo strobes pulsing back and forth along the hillside where the friendlies are dug in for the night. Wave upon wave of stuttering death ripple and crash through the dark, throwing unseen torrents of rock and dirt into the sky until, at last, even the explosions are snuffed in the pall. It's a Disneyland light show gone mad. Red globs streak away into the void, traveling north to south, and occasionally one bends at right angles skyward to waffle off into the night. The radio is alive with shouts, some with information, some for help, but all with the dismay that accompanies a sudden onslaught.

In the confusion it is tempting to focus on the impact area, but already your AO has picked up the mortars on the FLIR and turned his attention to plotting their location on his map.

"It'll take air to get them. There's a 7,000-foot mountain between them and the artillery."

"Okay, you relay their position while I scrounge up some air."

It will take twelve minutes for the Harriers standing strip alert to launch and arrive over the target, but there's a flight of A-4s standing by on Combat Air Patrol at Orbit Point Delta. DASC has already vectored them toward Foxtrot, an initial point located nine miles from the target at the south end of the valley. They can attack the mortar position in less than five minutes.

Suddenly the friendlies' hillside is awash in illumination flares, dozens popping open overhead in a nearly continuous stream.

"Argon from Lampshade, they're moving to the attack."

The mortar fire, which had coalesced along the forward edge of the friendly positions, begins to drift slowly south.

"Hostage Cow, this is Ripcord estimating Foxtrot in two minutes. We're a pair of Alpha-fours with twelve rockeyes and twenty mike-mike for your control."

"Keep it coming, Ripcord. We've got you some live ones."

Hastily, you go through your brief, covering ingress, target location and elevation, attack heading, friendly and enemy dispositions, target marking and egress. Friendly mortars have begun to range the area, so you arrange for a check fire (artillery pause) thirty seconds prior to Ripcord's estimated time on target. In the back, the AO has kept up a steady dialogue with Argon and Lampshade, requesting blue illumination on the front lines just prior to the air strike, which is designated to parallel the friendly positions, going from east to west and pulling off to the south.

With ninety seconds to target time, you turn in for your marking run, approaching from the southwest at 320 knots. At a mile and a half, you bring the nose up forty-five degrees above the horizon, and leading with right rudder as the airspeed decays below 200 knots, you draw the stick aft and to the right into the stop at its five o'clock position. Without a firm horizon, you switch your scan to the attitude gyro. Looking first for the wing symbols to parallel the white-black horizon terminator, you center the stick and rudders, and then as the black (you're pointing toward the dirt portion of the indicator) advances down thirty degrees below the center of the gauge, you tap a little forward stick and flick it full right, countering it with a half deflection of opposite rudder. Back again wings-level and in balanced flight with the pipper resting 500 meters north of the friendlies, you pickle off three "Willie-Pete" flares at two-second intervals before warping back around to the south. All three open at minimum altitude, and with the last one dropped leading the way, they land and continue emitting nearly a million candlepower while burning on the ground.

"Ripcord One, aim halfway between the center

flare and the one on the left. Dash Two, lay your's just north of the right flare."

"Tallyho the flares, Cow. Ripcord One is thirty seconds out." Almost simultaneously, the AO has called for a check fire.

From a distance the rockeyes look like a bunch of Fourth of July sparklers shimmering gaily against a black backdrop. It holds no such magic for those in the beaten zone. When it is properly delivered, there is no sanctuary for all who are above ground. A stick of six canisters can denude a twenty-acre plot of every living thing, displacing as much volume as a medium-size bush. The men in the open fare poorly indeed. Almost before the dust from the first runs settles, you've arced a pair of 2.75-inch rocket pods into the mortar position, and the

Skyhawks are back around pouring 20mm cannon fire into the melee. As Dash Two calls off, an AV-8 flight reports in, estimating Foxtrot in three minutes.

It has been less than ten minutes since the attack commenced, and although there is still a great deal of confusion on the ground, the assault has been stopped in its tracks. For several minutes more, mortar rounds thump sporadically into friendly positions, but after a second section of AV-8s unloads on its position, the last of the mortars fall silent, and what's left of the enemy forces scatters, retreating to the north in disarray.

"Argon, this is Hostage Cow. There's a pair of Hueys inbound for medevac. Standing by for casualty report."

Sea Knight (CH-46e)

Despite the fact that it has only three legs, it really does look like a Frog, especially sitting in a nose-high hover over a lily-patch. Boeing Vertol's CH-46 is getting old and the Corps is already itching to get its replacement (V-22 Osprey, of which more will be said in the next chapter), but since its introduction into the arsenal in 1964, it has been the Marines' workhorse in the assault troop transport business. With an empty weight of 12,500 pounds, the CH-46E can carry eighteen combat-loaded troops or 4,200 pounds of cargo 100 nautical miles at 120 knots. This may not sound impressive when you think of the CH-53's incredible stats, but you have to understand that this bird can do things no other aircraft would dare attempt. It is nimble and quick and rugged, able to get in (and back out of) landing zones that will boggle your mind. In the final analysis, the Frog is one of those happy things that now

Above: Crew chief eyeballs zone as CH-46 "Frog" drops in.

Right: Marines move out from their Frogs in sunrise attack exercise at Twentynine Palms.

and then occurs . . . a contraption that outdoes its specs and seems to get stronger and better with age.

It's been around for so long there's a temptation to dismiss it as an anachronism, but nothing could be further from the truth. For certain, the airframes are getting old, but in its latest configuration (E-model with ECM, crashworthy seats, and composite rotor blades, to name a few of the refinements), it's had a new lease on life. While it won't win the trophy dash on the straightaways—135 knots is pushing it to the limit—it more than makes up for its lack of blazing speed with its maneuverability in and around LZs. What is most surprising is how smooth and responsive it is, even in rough air, and when it comes to absorbing battle damage, it still ranks with the best.

When you get hauled out of your rack with only three hours' sleep after logging twelve hours during the day (a total violation of crew rest doctrine, but war has its own priorities), you know some-thing big is going down. The operations tent is packed with four Frog crews, two more from the CH-53 squadron, two pairs of gunship guys, the group commander, and an infantry light colonel who's about to open things off. The atmosphere is electric.

"We haven't much time, so here goes. Three days ago we learned that the enemy has taken over a pumping station that was manned by foreign engineers, two of whom are Americans. As near as we can tell, there are twelve of them being held hostage, and they've got them locked up in one of the pump houses."

As the story unfolds, you see the need for haste. The latest information is that the hostages are about to be transferred to a prison just outside the enemy's capital, nearly 600 miles away. The compound is guarded by perhaps as many as ten soldiers armed with automatic weapons, and though there is no evidence that they have antiaircraft

weapons, you've got to be prepared. The pumping station is a remote outpost in the middle of a broad and desolate valley. The nearest settlement—barely a wide spot in the road —is more than fifty miles to the east, and the nearest military facility is a hundred miles beyond.

Because of the urgency, the plan is simple. While you and the other CH-46s go to the brigade headquarters to embark a forty-man weapons platoon, the CH-53Es and Cobras will head north toward the pumping station to set up FARPs. Because the distance from the brigade area to the target is 225 nautical miles, two FARPs at 100 and 190 miles out will be set up so that if either Super Stallion goes down, the mission can still be accomplished. The total fuel for the round trip for the Frogs and Cobras is 25,000 pounds, 12,000 of which will be aboard the CH-53 at the farther point. With a target time of 0600, you'll launch at 0300, pick up troops at 0330 and, staying below 1,000 feet en route, proceed as two independent sections with ten-minute intervals to the FARPs. At 0535, with the Cobras in the lead, you'll dash to the compound, break your way in, rescue the engineers, and retire out

the same route. You'll have fighter cover the whole way, though its CAP station will be located forty miles west so as not to give your location away. The whole mission, until reaching the objective, will be carried out in radio silence.

There's a hush on the flight line as the eight aircraft are put through their final preparations. Bladders inside the CH-53s have been filled and the aircraft preflighted. As with the Cobras and CH-46s, an extra aircraft has been readied in case one of the primary birds goes down before launch. Litters and medical supplies have been loaded aboard each of the Frogs in case they're needed, and the grunts will have two corpsmen with them to provide first aid. At 0240, the Cobras start their turn-up. Because the Super Studs are faster, the attack birds will takeoff ten minutes earlier to arrive at the first FARP at the same time.

At 0245, you fire the auxiliary gas turbine power unit in preparation for main engine light off. Directing impingement air to the left engine, you watch as it comes up to 25 percent rpm before moving the condition lever into the ground idle detent. Immediately the exhaust gas temperature gauge leaps from the peg and mounts swiftly to 750 degrees. The whine of the turbine increases steadily until the engine stabilizes at 55 percent and 575 degrees. Both you and the copilot are deep into the checklists as you switch air to the right engine and monitor for the same values of temperature and rpm. After performing cyclic and directional control checks, you engage the rotors, which are interconnected through a central syncshaft. The aircraft goes through several stages of vibrations as the rotors come up to speed, but they dampen out once things are stabilized. One by one, systems are checked for proper performance and placed in their takeoff condition. The SAS (stability augmentation system) and functions of the automatic flight controls are cycled, and by the completion of the pretakeoff checklist, all the telelight panel warning lights are off. The crew chief, who has been outside the air-

Frogs hold tight echelon formation near Yuma.

craft monitoring the checks, climbs aboard, coiling his intercom line to keep it from fouling, and after he confirms his readiness for flight with a thumbs up, you turn your attention to the other three aircraft, awaiting the illumination of their anticollision beacons that indicate that they too are ready to go. Two minutes before launch, you turn on your beacon and taxi onto the roadway, where you'll perform your last checks, and as the digital clock on your knee board displays 0259:50, you add collective and forward cyclic and commence a running takeoff. It's not a takeoff in the fixed-wing sense, but rather a means of developing some translational lift before you add collective and fly it out of ground effect into the air.

The others are with you, lights out with four to six rotors' diameters separation between aircraft. Your wingman (number two) is off your right side at your four-thirty position, while three and four are out of your sight, balanced on the left side aligned on a forty-five degree bearing and stepped slightly up. At the brigade headquarters, the troops are split up into four groups for loading aboard the aircraft. While the birds are again topped off with fuel, gear and equipment are stowed, and at 0330 you and your wingman are again airborne, leaving the other section to await its interval.

The mission commander is aboard your bird and hooked into the intercom so that he can keep abreast of how things are going. Timing is critical because H-hour is set to take advantage of sunrise. The heading from the second FARP will take you slightly east of the pumping station, so that the final run-in will be on a heading of 330 degrees, putting you directly up-sun from the enemy. It seems like a trivial thing, but it's one more advantage, and there's no need to toss it away. The Cobras will dash in to keep the enemy pinned down while the Frogs land and disgorge their troops. Three of the birds will land outside of the compound while the fourth (yours) will land inside the fence. The main body will lay down a base of fire while the troops from

your chopper get to the prisoners to protect them. As soon as the troops are clear, you're to retire until the compound has been secured. The whole idea is to come in quickly with excessive force and blow hell out of any opposition. If there are prisoners to take, well and good, but first things first.

The Cobras have already departed as you arrive at the first FARP. Hoses are stretched from the 2,000-gallon bladder in the CH-53s belly to a stationary 485-gallon-per-minute gasoline engine-driven pump and from there to a single-point refueling nozzle for each CH-46. Though the rotors are stopped, the engines are still turning. Hook-up, checkout, transferring 1,250 pounds of fuel, and disengagement take less than four minutes per bird. As soon as the nozzles and ground wires are removed, you engage the rotors and complete your takeoff checklist. Just as you and your wingman become airborne, the second section breaks into a hover and settles in to take its drink. It's a tight schedule, but it cuts down on the amount of wasted fuel.

There's a twenty-minute wait after you've finished your second refueling before it's time to launch

Magnificent wood-truss hangar built to house Navy dirigibles at MCASH Tustin is now home for CH-46s of HMM-268.

for the target. The troops use the time for checking their weapons and gear, while you go over the route, tactics, and emergency procedures with the other crew in what is known as a "Zippo" brief. It's ten minutes to sunrise when you lift off for the target, which is twenty minutes away. As the FARP falls behind, you feel your insides doing flip-flops, and everything seems to be happening too fast. You're playing "catch-up," and the thought of that makes things worse. But it passes, and you're up on the front side of the power curve again with your mind and nerves under control.

As you turn to the final attack heading, you pass the lead to your number three (second section lead) and drop back into a two-mile trail, allowing you to come straight-in a minute later than the others, giving the troops time to take control of the fire tempo. With a little luck, by the time anyone knows you're there, you hope to have dumped your troops and breezed out of the zone.

"There's fire coming from the central building."

"Rog, I've got it." For the first time in the mission radio silence is broken.

"Okay, the troops are out. Let's clear the landing zone."

Smoke is rising from one of the buildings, and already a pall lies over the area. The Cobras dart in and out of the melee adding a swirling madness to the scene. Clumps of dirt fly up in the center of the compound, and you can hear the heaving volume of fire coming from the friendlies as you roar in above them and haul back on the cyclic to break into a low hover. That's what makes the Frog the best aircraft around for working a zone. You can come charging up at full tilt, sock the nose into the vertical, nail the collective, and stop it right now. Try that in almost any other transport and you'll overshoot. There's just a slight shudder as the airspeed bleeds off, and then, thump! Your tailwheels hit the ground, and before the nosewheel touches,

the troops are unstrapped and sprinting down the open ramp before peeling off for the pump house thirty meters to the right.

"Clear!" shouts the crew chief, and the collective is on its way up. It's going like clockwork. The ripping sound of small arms fire soars above the thrum of the blades as they bite the air, literally wrenching the aircraft off the ground. With this kind of timing and teamwork, they'll have the place secured in . . . wham wham wham wham . . . gabang! Lights you've never seen before except in the simulator come on like a pinball machine gone nuts. White, amber, red, they're all accounted for in a dazzling display of warning lights you'd have as soon missed. The aircraft stumbles, halts, sags, and in a flash of insight you realize that you're not going anywhere, buster, except down.

Secure this mother . . . engine condition levers back . . . rotor brake on . . . master off.

"Head for the pump house," you yell at the crew chief and copilot, but they don't need any encouragement. For an instant you sit there wondering what it is you've forgotten to do—"probably the most important thing," you tell yourself—and then you're out of your seat and into the cabin, which is awash with oil and hydraulic fluid pouring from the overhead.

"Don't go anywhere," you tell the still shuddering beast as you catch your leg on the cockpit aft bulkhead, and then, leaping from the starboard hatch, you dash across the courtyard, crouched low against an imaginary hail of fire.

The fight is over before you reach the pump house but you're so deep in your one-track mode that you don't realize it until you nearly collide with half a dozen troops as they sweep by, searching for more enemy soldiers. Seven captives are herded out into the courtyard where they are searched, while one by one, the bodies of another six soldiers are laid out in the lee of the main building. Surprisingly, except for a few cuts and bruises, the Marines have sustained no casualties, and the engineers, beyond

The ungainly looking Frog has given the Marine Corps yeoman service for two decades. It will be replaced in the '90s by the JVX "Osprey" tilt-rotor transport.

being scared and confused, are fine. The whole engagement has taken less than five minutes since the Cobras first opened up, yet the flow of individual images that well up in the sudden quiet seem to stretch back in time forever.

The other choppers return and land, and the crews come over to look at the damage to yours. The skin on the right side of the rear rotor mast has been torn away revealing the mangled gizzards of engine and power train. There are holes in the cabin as well, but they're of no real concern. This bird's going nowhere under its own power and the thought of having to abandon her in this barren patch of desert leaves you with a feeling of emptiness. It's like the movies with the cowboy about to dispatch his fallen mount, but before you have a chance to think about lighting a match to it, word comes that the CH-53 from the second FARP is inbound to top off the other birds and lift yours back to the base.

That's what they call *flexibility*.

Chapter 6
The Nineties and Beyond

There are other scenarios—other ways Marine Air might (indeed, will) be employed in a tactical situation—but the role of Marine Air is the same. It is there to support infantry operations right down to the point of fixing bayonets and (perish the thought) slogging it out in the mud. All Marine tactical aircraft are capable of working from carriers, so the operations originating at either the rear or forward base could as well have been launched from a pitching flight deck as from a piece of concrete. What should be obvious is that aviation is integral to all aspects of the ground scheme of maneuver, and in the literal sense, air units will be the first on the scene, reconnoitering, prepping, or pathfinding.

Underlying the direct applications of the various aircraft and their contributions to the overall role of Marine Air is a broader area of understanding of the implications of such a potpourri of capabilities. It would be nice if you could define the tasks to which Marine Air might be used because you could make drastic cuts in the types and mix of aircraft, but it is precisely the open-ended nature of the task that mandates its complexity. What is interesting is that while the roster of aircraft has been slow to change, the roles of the aircraft themselves show no such permanence. A case in point is the OV-10 which began life as a lightly armed reconnaissance aircraft, but over the years Marines have adapted it to a far broader range of missions than its designers ever dreamed possible. The truth is that for every challenge there is a response, and for Marine aviators, steeped in the "can do" tradition, this often means "make do" with whatever is at hand rather than start from ground zero.

If there is a discernable direction within Marine Air that is different from other branches—indeed something of a new departure within the Corps—it is in bringing air as close to the battlefield as possible. The emergence of the attack helicopter is the most obvious example of this, also the OV-10. The day of the Harrier is just now dawning, and there is little doubt that there will be teething problems for perhaps years to come. But if the final configuration of a tactical STOVL aircraft is in doubt, its battlefield potential is not. Marine Air today is more flexible than it has ever been, but the future holds more promise than we can begin to envision.

How different will Marine Air look as we head into the last decade of the century? Not much, it seems, unless something momentous—another war or rampant peace—rears its head in the next couple of years, in which case all bets are off. What we have seen over the last two decades is a shift toward a force composed of fewer, more capable aircraft, with an emphasis in the last several years on increased reliability of the total system. SLEPs account for the serviceability of a large number of aircraft, some of which are nearly as old as the people who fly them. For the active duty fixed-wing forces, present plans call for the gradual re-

The Beech C-12, similar to the civilian King Air, is used by several military branches as an executive transport and multi-engine trainer.

placement of A-4s by AV-8s and F-4s by F/A-18s, the former to be accomplished by 1992 and the latter by the end of the century. Vagaries in the funding train will no doubt cause these dates to change (slide, unless you believe in the tooth fairy), but it isn't likely that the Corps will see momentous changes in the fighter and daylight attack world before the twenty-first century.

There are some unknowns in the fixed-wing community, such as replacements for RF-4s, A-6Es, and EA-6Bs. There is mounting pressure from within to go entirely to two-seater F/A-18s to replace all three. Champions of this approach point out that by increasing the total buy of F/A-18s, the unit cost will decrease, creating a considerable savings. Moreover, because the variants would have such a high degree of commonality, there would be enormous savings in equipment and parts support as well as in training costs, not only for air

crews, but support personnel as well. The major objection to the mostly common two-seater Hornet (aside from the obvious loss to competitive manufacturers) is that if you come up with a critical design deficiency in the future, you run the risk of having your entire fleet grounded at the same time.

Proponents of the two-seater in the tactical community argue that despite the advantages of the displays and systems in the aircraft, the F/A-18 pilot is right up there in the overload mode the minute the sky starts to fill with airplanes. Keeping oriented in maneuvering flight takes full concentration, leaving the pilot no time to look at and evaluate the data his displays are giving him. The beauty of the Phantom has always been in the division of duties its two-seat configuration affords, and although the weapons system itself is not as advanced, nor is the aircraft as nimble as the latest generation of MiG gobblers, the extra set of eyeballs is a great equalizer once the turning begins. (There is probably an objection to this line of reasoning, but I haven't heard one that's worth sour owl droppings, if you'll pardon a little wishy-washiness.)

On the rotary-wing side of the house, a bunch of things are going on. First, there's the continuing need to upgrade and expand the attack helicopter fleet. Present plans call for the purchase of forty-four AH-1T(Plus) Cobras in two 22-plane increments, beginning in fiscal year 1985. Additionally, a study is being conducted on the feasibility of adapting the Hughes AH-64 Apache attack helicopter to meet Marine specifications. It may not seem so—particularly to those who are in the midst of it—but helicopter attack is really in its infancy. As capabilities increase and experience in the field accumulates, new requirements are generated at an ever increasing rate. It's almost like fixed-wing aviation in the forties and fifties, when the development rate went supercritical.

Without a doubt, the most innovative program going is the V-22 Osprey, the tilt-wing replacement for the CH-46E. Scheduled for delivery beginning in 1991, the Bell/Boeing vertical-lift medium transport will be a radical departure from what has come before. Let's look at it from a conceptual standpoint for just a moment. In the CH-53 section, we talked about the difference between hovering flight and translational flight—how in the former case the bite of the blade remains constant throughout its sweep, whereas in forward flight the blade angle has to be constantly changed to compensate for differences in the speed at which the blade meets the air. Well, the tilt-wing solves the problem differently. In the vertical mode, it's a helicopter, the two propellers acting like dual rotors to draw the aircraft into the sky. Transition to forward flight is accomplished by rotating the propellers forward until they are perpendicular to the ground. At this point, the aircraft is in conventional flight. If you want to go back into a hover, you reverse the process, tilting the blades until they are once again parallel to the ground. Think of what this means: The aircraft can operate out of an unprepared area, takeoff and land vertically just like a helo, accelerate (or decelerate) like gangbusters, maneuver right down there in the weeds, turn on a dime to bring its weapons to bear on a target, cruise far more efficiently than any other helicopter of its lifting capacity ever could, and run like stink when the time comes.

The Osprey will be the first wholly composite aircraft ever built for the military—there will be some metal substructures, but 90 percent will be plastic—and it will sport a built-in digital data bus with fly-by-wire controls. Right from the first, it will be configured with a cannon, Sidewinder missiles, external stores attach points, and a refueling probe. For shipboard use, it will fold away almost within its own length. Visualize this: After landing with the props in the helicopter mode, the blades are hydraulically folded inboard along the wingline, after which the pods are rotated forward to the normal flight position. Then (and this is a grab-

Marine fighter pilots are represented on the faculty of Top Gun, the Navy Fighter Weapons School. Top Gunners use the Northrop F-5E to simulate enemy fighters like the Soviet MiG 21.

ber) the whole wing is rotated ninety degrees clockwise (viewed from above) putting the left pod in front of the cockpit like a lazy Susan.

There are other things. The length of the blades allows the propellers to be turned slowly, which in turn quiets them beyond belief. The use of composites not only eases the manufacturing process, it permits easier and cheaper repair of battle-damaged panels. It can haul troops and cargo. It can perform medevac and SAR missions. It can protect itself in the battlefield environment and do CAS when needed. In all, it's a hell of a prospect.

The aircraft themselves are one thing, and to a great extent they and the mission are the drivers for the procurement of subsystems, but there are technological advances in other fields that will have an important impact on Marine aviation. For instance, before the development of lightweight night vision goggles and high resolution infrared displays, much of the night work that can now be done would have been suicidal. It seems safe to assume that work in this area will receive ever greater attention, and this in turn will have an impact on Marine Air's mission.

For those reared in the vacuum tube and transistor era, the present displays are amazing, but they have only begun to make their presence felt. The microchip offers such colossal advances in what the aircraft can do that you end up being overwhelmed by its infinite potential. The problem isn't just one for the whiz kids at Hughes or the program managers at Naval Air Systems Command; it is one that works its way into the cockpit. No matter how

fast you can feed data to the HUD or screen, the main processor in the aircraft assimilates information at the same rate it did when its user rattled around the jungle looking for someone to thump with a stick. There isn't time in a tactical environment for the pilot to go through a long list of options of what's available to him in the gizmo. He's going to go with what he's most comfortable with, and if it doesn't tell him exactly what he needs to know, he'll cover for the difference. The point is

Right: Another air-ground team is composed of the men who fly the machines and those who maintain them. Their pride, skill, and devotion to duty are the enduring ingredients of Marine Air.

The amazing V-22 Osprey, a combination of rotary-wing flexibility and fixed-wing speed, will become the primary Marine troop transport in the '90s.

that unless you can positively guarantee before the fact just what situation is going to present itself at any given moment, or unless someone finds a way to use the pilot's perception to call up the appropriate display, the presentations will remain proximate—better by far than what didn't exist before, but far short of their potential. With that caveat, it is still possible to speculate on the kinds of things integrated circuits might do in the future.

When the firing starts, command, control, and communications (C-cubed) are the most critical elements and typically those that are the most degraded. TAOC (tactical air operations control)-85 is a major program aimed at modernizing the Marine Corps's air control system. When it is installed and made operational, it will be a quantum leap over the present system, yet it too will suffer from the same things that have plagued its predecessors overload and confusion in the heat of battle. There's nothing new about this. If Caesar had had the latest model equipment, he still wouldn't have conquered the world. Somewhere along the way, something would have gotten garbled, and Gaul would have ended up in four parts, not three. Still,

you have to believe that if there is any area that will benefit from advancing chip technology, it will be C-cubed.

Great strides have been made in airborne positioning and navigation systems. The inertial nav in the AV-8B is good to within a 1,000 feet after a half hour of flight—plenty good for most applications, but wholly unsatisfactory for conventional ordnance delivery. Even at ten times the accuracy, it would be of marginal utility for providing primary information for bombing; you have to believe that the need is there for a system even ten times better than that. One shudders at the thought of star trackers, or board after board of pattern recognition chips–PROMs for every fifteen minute chart in the world (egad)—but maybe there is a far simpler or more elegant solution.

ECM. Lord knows how many bucks have gone into the little black boxes that fill every uncommitted nook and cranny of our tactical aircraft, but it's safe to assume that we "ain't seen nothin' yet." Trying to hide an aircraft from prying eyes—particularly when you're coming onto enemy turf with mayhem in mind—is a tough proposition, yet clearly

it will remain among the highest priorities. Heretofore, this has meant truckloads of little green pictures of dead presidents flowing down some hidden rat hole, but with the exorbitant cost of nearly everything having to do with fielding a fighting force, we are long overdue in rethinking our entire Defense Department procurement philosophy. And there's no better place to start than the world of ECM.

There's probably some ratio between the number of dollars spent and the time and level of confusion you can throw into the game, which would suggest that beyond a certain point you're stroking yourself. Our approach has been to start at the megabuck level and work up, while the Israelis totally mystified the Syrians by launching a bunch of model airplanes into their airspace. When the smoke cleared, the score read SAMs launched -57, Israeli aircraft downed—O. Model airplanes are reasonably cheap expendables unless you try to make them do everything under the sun by calling them RPVs (remotely piloted vehicles) so you can jack the unit cost up. Chaff bundles and flares are cheaper still. With the new materials and present-day microminiaturization techniques, there ought to be a lot of clever ways to approach the ECM problem without it costing an arm and a leg. The development of low-cost expendable "smart" chaff comes to mind as among the many existing possibilities.

Not that ECM manufacturers are "bad guys"— they aren't. There is a valid need for their gear, and certainly Marines profit from the effort. But Marine requirements differ from those of the Air Force and the Navy. Marines aren't looking to create hundred-mile corridors; they are trying to throw up a curtain just long enough to get in, drop their ordnance, and breeze it. Sure, they'd like to keep the enemy deaf, dumb, and blind forever, but they don't *need* to. The problem is that more than anyone, Marines suffer from the high costs of equipment. Real choices have to be made, and the trade-offs are rarely palatable. Sure you need ECM, but at what price? Is the marginal increase in protection worth as much as increased accuracy at the target, if (for instance) the trade-off were that you had to go back a second or perhaps third time to do the job? Would a lesser ECM capability be offset by retrofitting older aircraft with better displays? Does the allocation of a large chunk of money for ECM research and development against a finite defense budget cut into the purchase of badly needed spares and replenishment items? And if so, is the trade-off a valid one? Marines will make do with whatever they're given because that's how they've always been, but these are the kinds of questions whose answers will shape the future of the MAGTF.

Appendix
United States Marine Corps
Organization Charts

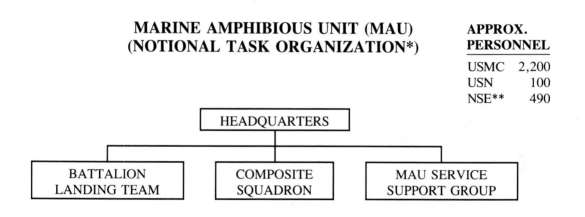

MARINE AMPHIBIOUS UNIT (MAU)
(NOTIONAL TASK ORGANIZATION*)

APPROX.
PERSONNEL

USMC	2,200
USN	100
NSE**	490

HEADQUARTERS

BATTALION LANDING TEAM · COMPOSITE SQUADRON · MAU SERVICE SUPPORT GROUP

AIRCRAFT/LAUNCHERS

12 CH-46
4 CH-53 A/D
2 CH-53E
8 AH-1[1]
4 UH-1
20 REDEYE/STINGER LAUNCHERS

MAJOR EQUIPMENT

5	TANKS	8	155MM HOW
8	81MM MORTAR	9	60MM MORTAR
32	DRAGON LAUNCHERS	20	50 CAL MG
8	TOW LAUNCHERS	60	M60 MG
12	AAV		

[1]THIS DET COULD BE REPLACED OR REINFORCED BY 1 VMA DET (6 AV-8) AS THE TACTICAL SITUATION DICTATES.

*ACTUAL TASK ORGANIZATION FORMED TO ACCOMPLISH SPECIFIC MISSIONS MAY VARY FROM THE ORGANIZATION SHOWN.

**NAVAL SUPPORT ELEMENT

MARINE AMPHIBIOUS BRIGADE (MAB)
(NOTIONAL TASK ORGANIZATION*)

APPROX.
PERSONNEL (AE)

USMC	11,200
USN	540
NSE**	1,250

BRIGADE HEADQUARTERS		
REGIMENTAL LANDING TEAM	MARINE AIRCRAFT GROUP	BRIGADE SERVICE SUPPORT GROUP

AIRCRAFT/LAUNCHERS

40	AV-8/A4	48	CH-46
24	F-4/F-18	32	CH-53A/D
20	A-6	10	CH-53E
7	EA-6	24	AH-1
4	RF-4	6	UH-1
6	OV-10	6	HAWK LAUNCHERS
8	KC-130	60	REDEYE/STINGER LAUNCHERS

MAJOR EQUIPMENT

17	TANKS	30	155MM HOW
24	81MM MORTAR	6	8″ HOW (SP)
96	DRAGON LAUNCHERS	27	60MM MORTAR
24	TOW LAUNCHERS	138	50 CAL MG
45	AAV	255	M-60 MG

*ACTUAL TASK ORGANIZATION FORMED TO ACCOMPLISH SPECIFIC MISSIONS MAY VARY CONSIDERABLY FROM THE ORGANIZATION SHOWN.

**NAVAL SUPPORT ELEMENT.

MARINE AMPHIBIOUS FORCE (MAF)
(NOTIONAL TASK ORGANIZATION*)

APPROX.
PERSONNEL (AE)

USMC	35,000
USN	1,600
NSE**	2,800

AIRCRAFT/LAUNCHERS		MAJOR EQUIPMENT	
100 AV-8/A-4	156 CH-46	70 TANKS	90 155MM HOW
72 F-4/F-18	80 CH-53A/D	72 81MM MORTAR	18 155MM HOW (SP)
40 A-6	72 AH-1	288 DRAGON LAUNCHERS	12 8″ HOW (SP)
15 EA-6	24 UH-1	72 TOW LAUNCHERS	81 60MM MORTAR
7 RF-4	32 CH-53E	208 AAV	435 50 CAL MG
12 OV-10	24 HAWK LAUNCHERS	601 M-60 MG	
24 KC-130	300 REDEYE/STINGER		
12 TA-4/OA-4	LAUNCHERS		

*ACTUAL TASK ORGANIZATION FORMED TO ACCOMPLISH SPECIFIC MISSIONS MAY VARY CONSIDERABLY FROM THE ORGANIZATION SHOWN.

**NAVAL SUPPORT ELEMENT.

Glossary

AAA: antiaircraft artillery—also known as triple-A

ACM: air combat maneuvering—fighter-versus-fighter stuff

AO: aviation officer

ARBS: angle rate bombing system—a computer-assisted weapons delivery aid that continuously computes the ballistic trajectory of free-fall weapons, allowing for their automatic release when the proper tracking solution has been achieved

AWLS: all-weather landing system—an aircraft system that takes a signal from a transmitter located at the landing site and displays glideslope and courseline information to the pilot

BN: bombardier/navigator—runs the weapons system in the A-6

BIT: built-in test—self-checking routines found in many electronic systems

C³: command, control, and communications—also called "C-cubed"

CAP: combat air patrol

CAS: close air support—any of a variety of fire support missions prosecuted in proximity to friendly positions, generally within 1,500 meters

CAX: combined arms exercise

DASC: direct air support center

DDI: digital display indicator

ECM: electronic countermeasures—a variety of active electronic jamming procedures

ELINT: electric intelligence—a variety of passive snooping on enemy electronic capabilities

FAC: forward air controller—an aviator assigned to a ground unit to assist in coordinating close air support strikes

FAC(A): forward air controller (airborne)

FARP: forward area refueling point—a remote filling station established by a KC-130 or CH-53 carrying a rubber fuel

FEBA: forward edge of the battle area

FLIR: forward looking infrared—detection units mounted in various aircraft to help distinguish targets at night

HOTAS: hands on throttle and stick—a cockpit configuration that allows the pilot to keep his hands where they belong during combat maneuvering

HST: helicopter support team—a ground detail assigned to support helicopter logistics operations

HUD: head up display—projection of flight and tactical information to a screen in the pilot's normal line of sight

INS: inertial navigation system—a system that maintains a plot of the aircraft's spatial position by measuring various inertial inputs and summing their vectors

IP: initial point—an arbitrary point over the ground used as a reference to a target

LAAM: light antiaircraft missile—refers to a Hawk missile battalion composed of several missile batteries and supporting elements

LID: lift improvement devices—modifications to the underside of the original AV-8A designed to cut down on losses to vectored-thrust lift characteristics

LOX: liquid oxygen—commonly converted to gaseous oxygen for breathing purposes

LPH: landing platform helicopter

LZ: landing zone—the designated site for a helicopter insert of troops and/or supplies

MAC: military airlift command—an Air Force element in charge of logistical transportation of men and equipment

MAG: Marine aircraft group—an intermediate level of command composed of a variety of combat and support squadrons

MAGTF: Marine air/ground task force—what the book is about

MAW: Marine aircraft wing—the basic element of Marine aviation, composed of several combat and support MAGs. It is the lowest self-sufficient element in Marine Air

MFD: multifunction display—any of a variety of cathode ray cockpit displays capable of presenting computer-generated symbology and data covering flight and combat conditions

RIO: radar intercept officer—the weapons system operator in the back seat of a Phantom (and perhaps the possible two-seat F/A-18)

SLEP: service life extension program—a rejuvenation program for aging aircraft

STOVL: short takeoff/vertical landing—a convolution of the more familiar VSTOL operational scheme that is more in keeping with the Harrier's true capabilities. It recognizes that vertical operations at high gross weights and/or density altitudes are currently impractical

Squadron Designations:
HMA Marine Attack Helicopter
HMH Marine Heavy Transport Helicopter
HMM Marine Medium Transport Helicopter
HMX Marine Experimental Helicopter
VMA Marine Attack

VMAT Marine Attack Training
VMAQ Marine Attack/Electronic Warfare
VMFA Marine Fighter/Attack
VMFAT Marine Fighter/Attack Training
VMFP Marine Fighter/Photo Reconnaissance
VMO Marine Observation VMGR Marine Air Refueling/Transport

TAOR: tactical area of responsibility—the territory over which a tactical commander exercises operational control

TOW: an antiarmor air-to-surface and surface-to-surface missile whose name derives from its characteristics -tube-mounted, optically tracked, wire-guided

TWS: track-while-scan—a capability of certain radars that allows them to "lock onto" targets while continuing in the search mode

VID: visual identification—a requirement when the identity of an aircraft is not known

VSTOL: vertical/short takeoff and landing.

WTI: weapons tactics instructor—a MAWTS-1 graduate

The Author

John Trotti was a Marine fighter pilot for 12 years, serving two tours of duty in Vietnam, where he flew over 600 missions. These Vietnam experiences are depicted in his book PHANTOM OVER VIETNAM (Presidio, 1983). Trotti is now a consulting engineer and writer, based in Santa Barbara, California.

The Photographer

George Hall is a San Francisco photographer specializing in aerial and aviation topics. He is co-author of THE BLIMP BOOK, WORKING FIRE: THE SAN FRANCISCO FIRE DEPARTMENT, and THE GREAT AMERICAN CONVERTIBLE. His photos illustrate the Presidio AIRPOWER books—CV: Carrier Aviation, USAFE: A Primer of Modern Air Combat in Europe, and RED FLAG: Air Combat for the '80s.